LADAKH
The Land of Gompas

From the sketchbook of
Slobodan Maldini

Slobodan Maldini

LADAKH
The Land of Gompas
From the sketchbook of Slobodan Maldini

Copyright, design and photographs copyright: ©Slobodan Maldini

Author and publisher: Slobodan Maldini

Book design by: Slobodan Maldini

Cover page: Namgyal Tsemo Gompa, Leh, by: Slobodan Maldini

First edition: 2017

All rights reserved.
No part of this book may be reproduced or transmitted in any form
or by means electronic or mechanical, including photocopying,
recording or by any information storage retrieval system,
without prior permission in written from the publisher Slobodan Maldini.

Project editor and designer: Slobodan Maldini

Slobodan Maldini
e-mail: maldini.slobodan@gmail.com

Printed by: CreateSpace, An Amazon.com Company

LADAKH
The Land of Gompas

From the sketchbook of Slobodan Maldini

LADAKH
The Land of Gompas

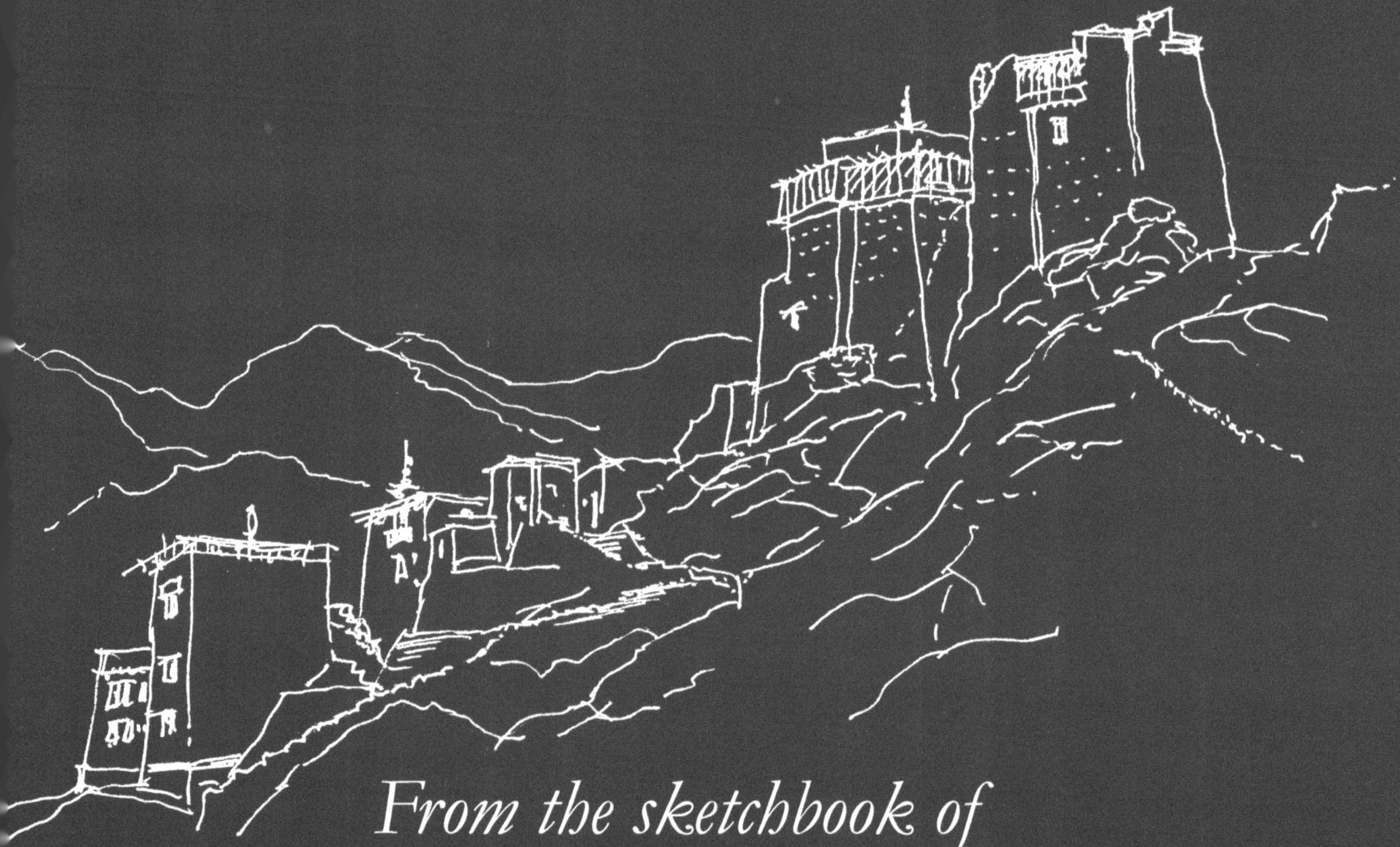

*From the sketchbook of
Slobodan Maldini*

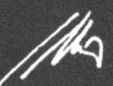

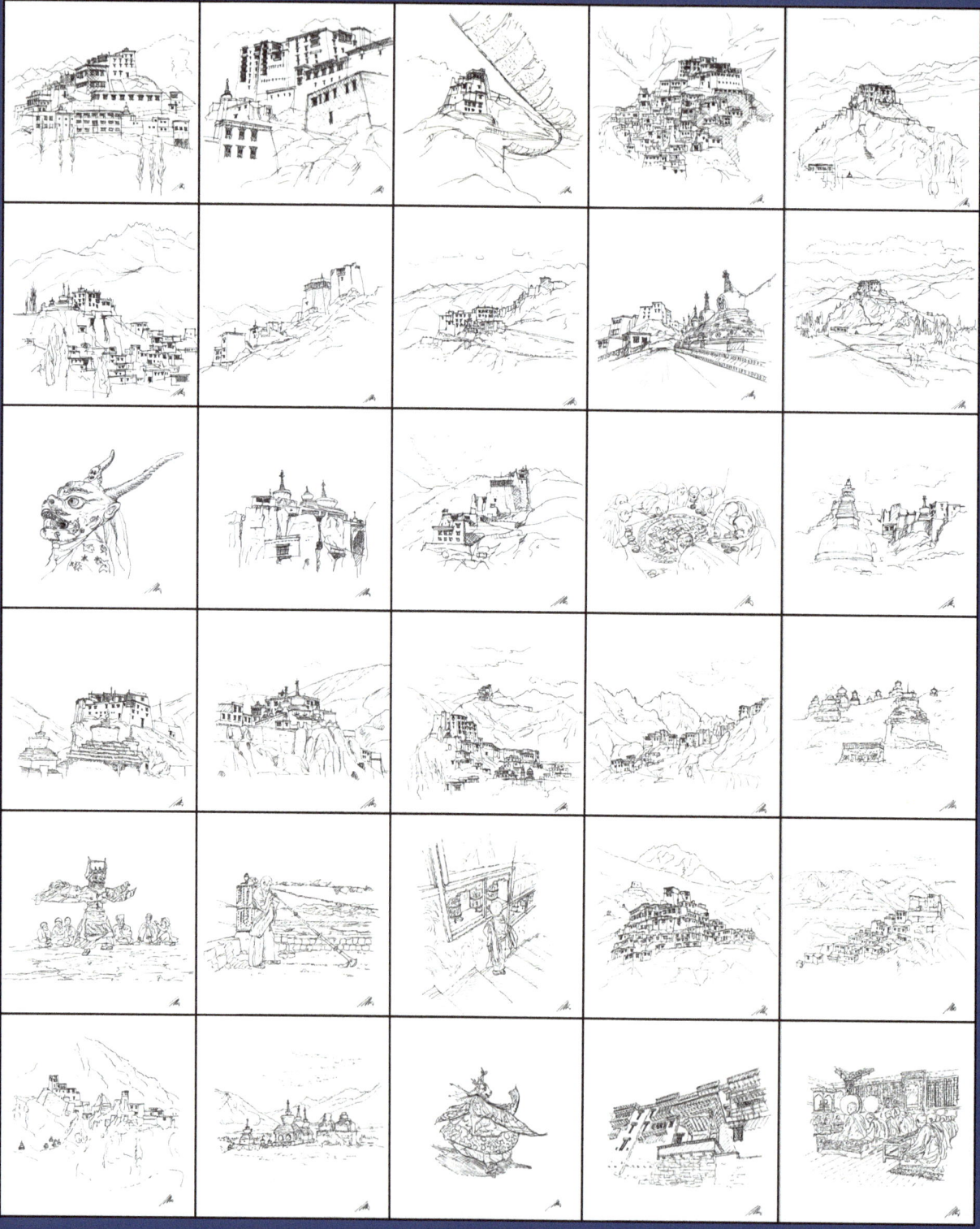

CONTENTS:

1 Thiksey Gompa
2 Spituk Gompa
3 Namgyal Tsemo Gompa, Leh
4 Chemrey Gompa
5 Stakna Gompa
6 Lamayuru Gompa
7 Namgyal Tsemo Gompa
8 Spituk Gompa
9 Thiksey Gompa
10 Stakna Gompa
11 Cham dance, masked monk, Tso Moriri lake
12 Lamayuru Gompa
13 Namgyal Gompa
14 Making mandala, kalachakra, Ladakh
15 Shey Old palace
16 Bardan Gompa, Zanskar
17 Lamayuru Gompa
18 Leh palace, Leh
19 Lamayuru Gompa
20 Stupas nearby Shey Gompa
21 Cham dance, Leh
22 Monk playing lawah - long trumpet
23 Boy monk at Thiksey Gompa
24 Diskit Gompa, Nubra valley
25 Diskit Gompa
26 Basgo Gompa
27 Buddhist stupas in Ladakh
28 Buddhist monk performing cham dance, Lamayuru Gompa
29 Shey palace, detail of architecture
30 Buddhist monks in meditation, Soma Gompa, Leh

The Land of Gompas

THE LAND OF GOMPAS

During the past decade I had a great dream to travel to Ladakh.

Under the title "The Book of Bodhisattva" I wrote my first book about the journey to Ladakh, the land of desert and mountains in the heart of Himalayas. In the book I described stay in Thiksey Gompa, near the town of Leh, and trek to the small, isolated and remote Himalayan mountain village. There I stayed thirty seven days in a small mountain cottage, where had the opportunity to read the famous Buddhist scripture "The Book of Bodhisattva." This short-term stay in Ladakh has made on me a big spiritual transformation. My life has changed from its roots.

Few years later, I made a series of sketches of Ladakh traditional architecture, and finally published them in this map of drawings. This artistic monograph shows thirty handmade drawings of Ladakh Buddhist Gompas. These sketches, made by ink on paper, represent a dozen outstanding Buddhist Gompas, drawn from the point of view of the pedestrian traveler. This book of drawings contains sketches of fascinating Himalayan architecture, *incredible medieval settlements, and the Buddhist monasteries that represent perfection of the skills of ancient builders in Ladakh. Although many of this Buddhist monasteries are in the process of disappearing, even collapse to ruins, they still leave an incredible impressions on the viewers. Primarily because they are exalted, spiritual spaces, also as the harbors of the unique spirituality and philosophy of Himalayan Buddhists.*

This book, a monograph and collection of travelogue sketches is a unique piece of art created by the hands of artist, architect, art historian, and most of all Buddhist Slobodan Maldini/ Karma Yeshe Gyatso. The drawings in the book are unique, authentic, made from the hand of a renowned artist - the connoisseur of Buddhism. They leave nobody indifferent. This unique collection of drawings is a valuable artistic and historical material that testifies to the incredible Himalayan Buddhists architecture.

LADAKH

Ladak is a region in North India in the state Jammu an Kashmir that extends between the Kunlun mountain range in the north and the Great Himalayas in the south, at altitudes above 3000m. Through the Ladakh flows the holy Indus River, which springs near the Lake Manasarovar under the holy Mount Kailash in the Tibetan Plateau, and represents the source of life in this area. The Ladakh space is called "Little Tibet," because is inhabited by the people of Tibet and the Indo-Aryan race. Ladakh was an important area of trade in the past, and today is the area where the population survives on the verge of existence. The biggest place in Ladak is Leh, the former capital of Ladakh. Ladakh's population consists of Muslims and Buddhists. They are engaged in cattle breeding and farming.

On the territory of Ladakh, are preserved many Buddhist monasteries, and Ladakh is known as "The Land of Gompas." Gompas are Buddhist fortified monasteries, centers of the transmission of Buddhist traditional teachings and spiritual practice, with dormitories and meditation halls for the monks. Every settlement, and even small village in Ladakh, has the Buddhist Gompa.

1. Gompa Thiksey

Tiksey Gompa is a Tibetan Buddhist monastery of the Gelugpa Order, also known as the Order of the Yellow Hats. Located about 19 km away from Leh, erected on the top of a hill above the village of Tiksey. Is famous for its similarity to the Potala Palace in Lassa and is one of the largest Gompa in central Ladakh. The gompa was built during the early 15th century.

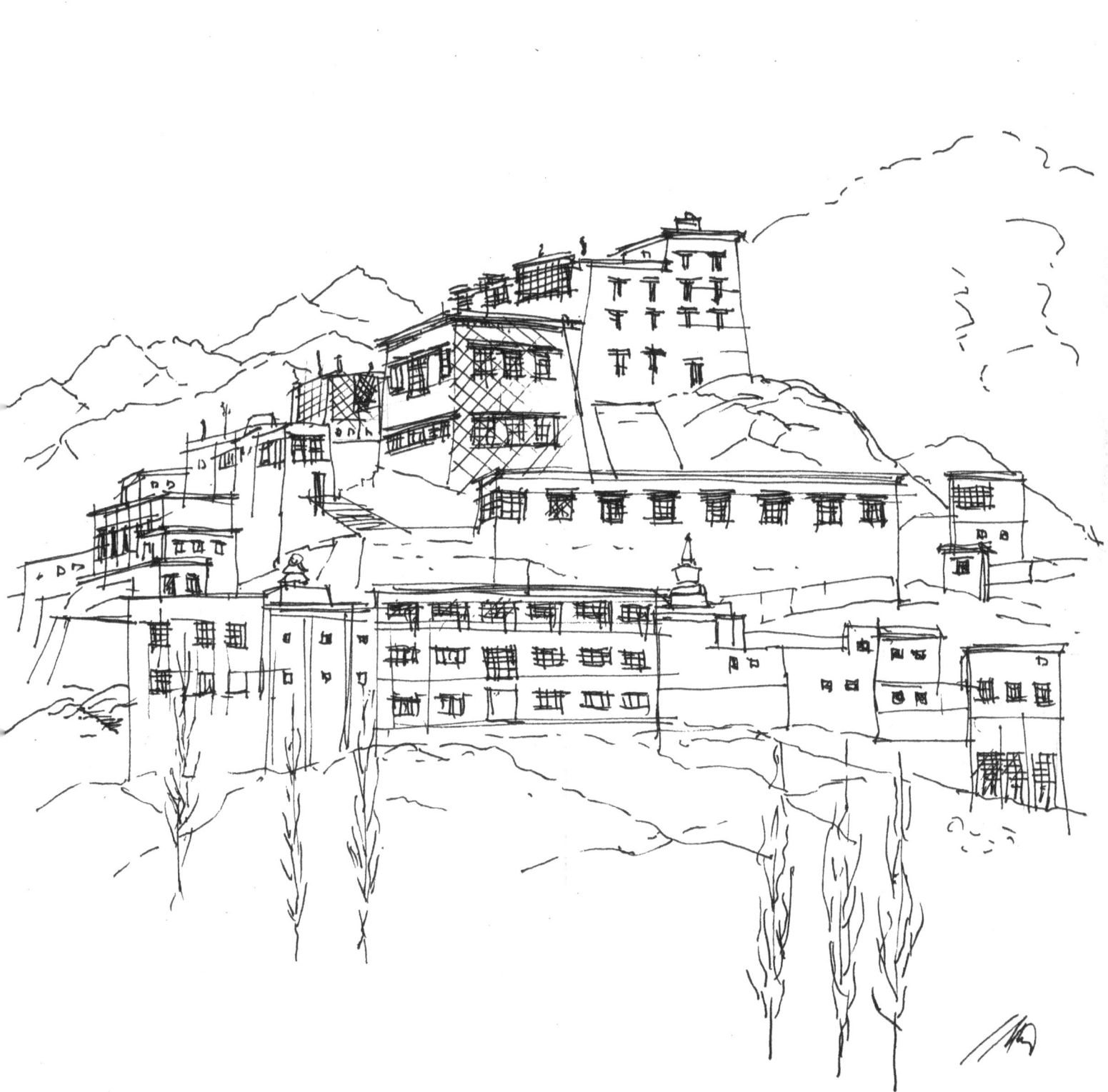

2. Spituk Gompa

Spituk Gompa is located at an elevation, 8 km from Leh. This monastery was founded in the 11th century by Buddhists of the Order Black Hats, and in the 15th century was taken over by the Buddhists of the Order of the Yellow Hats

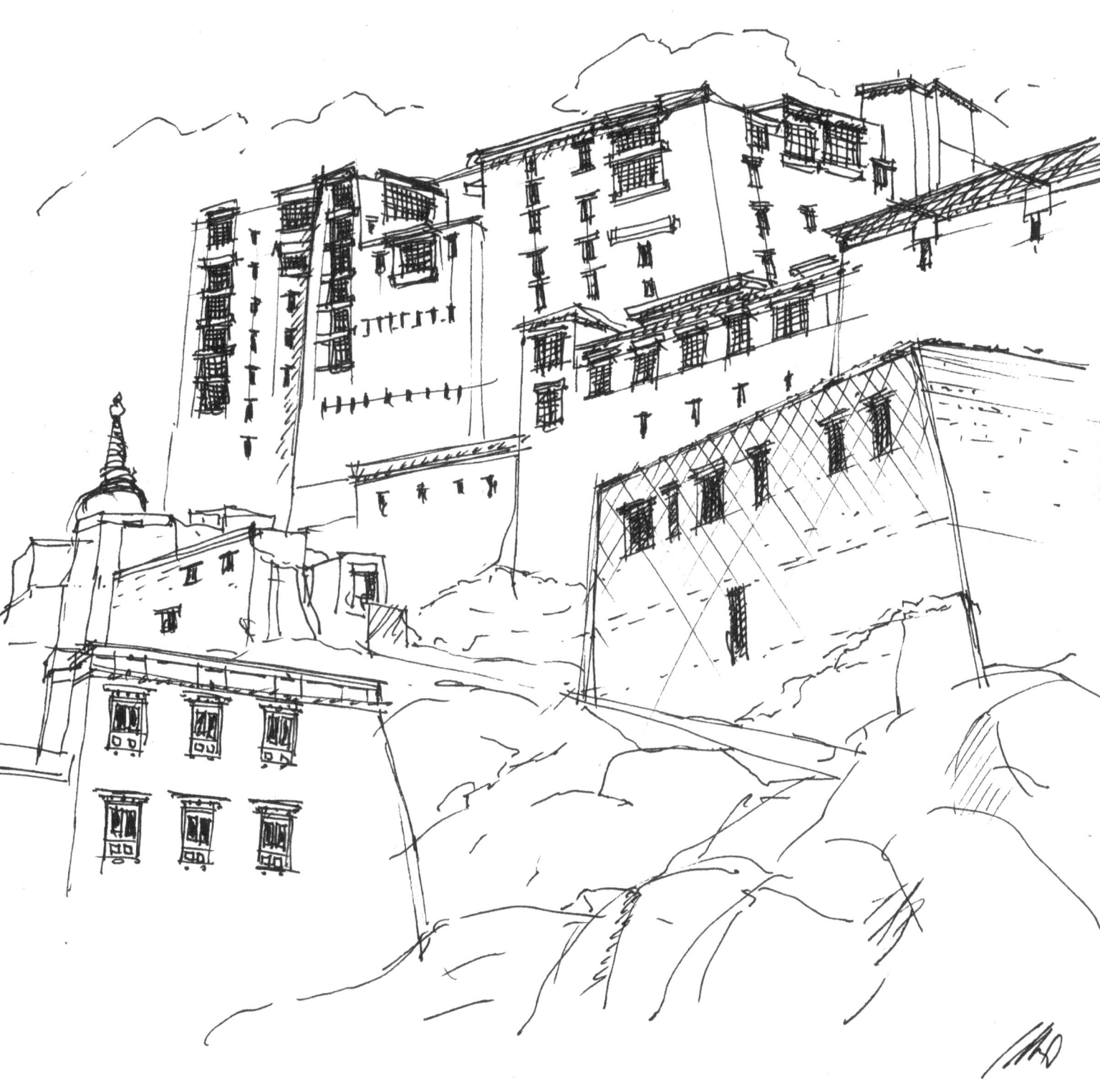

3. Namgyal Tsemo gompa

The Buddhist monastery Namgyal Tsemo was built on the hill above the city of Leh in 1430. King Tashi Namgyal, a great follower of Buddhism, as a sign of respecting Buddhism, built a gompa on Namgyal hill above his palace. Below the hill stands the Shankar gompa, connected to the monastery above.

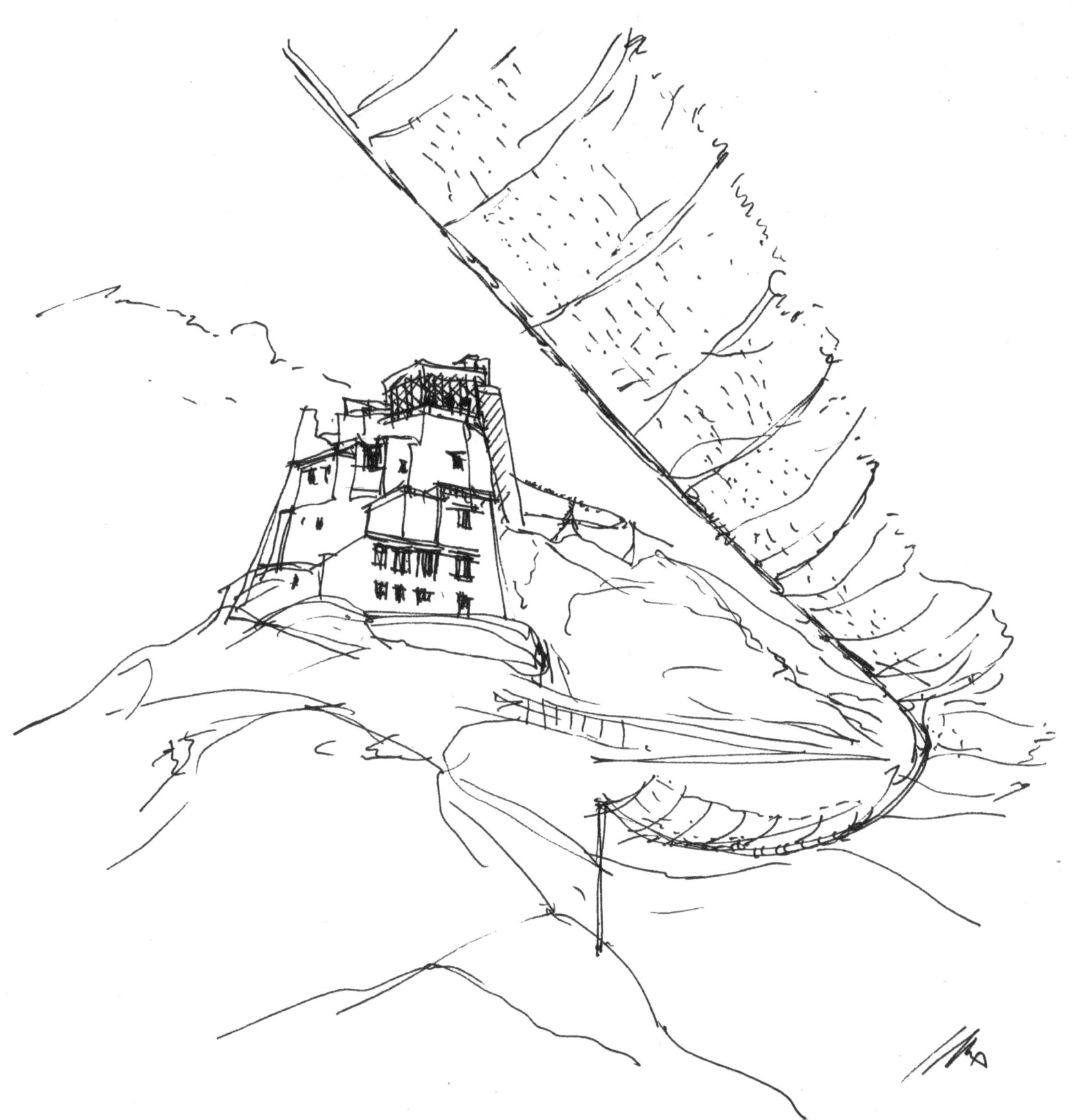

4. Chemrey monastery

The Buddhist pilgrimage Chemrey is located about 40 km east of Leh, and belongs to the Drugpa Buddhist Order or "Red Hat Order," the Kagyu school branch of Tibetan Buddhism. Was founded in 1664 by Lama Tagsang Raschen dedicated to the King Senhgge Namgyal. Every year, the festival of holy dance Chemrey Angchok is held in the monastery.

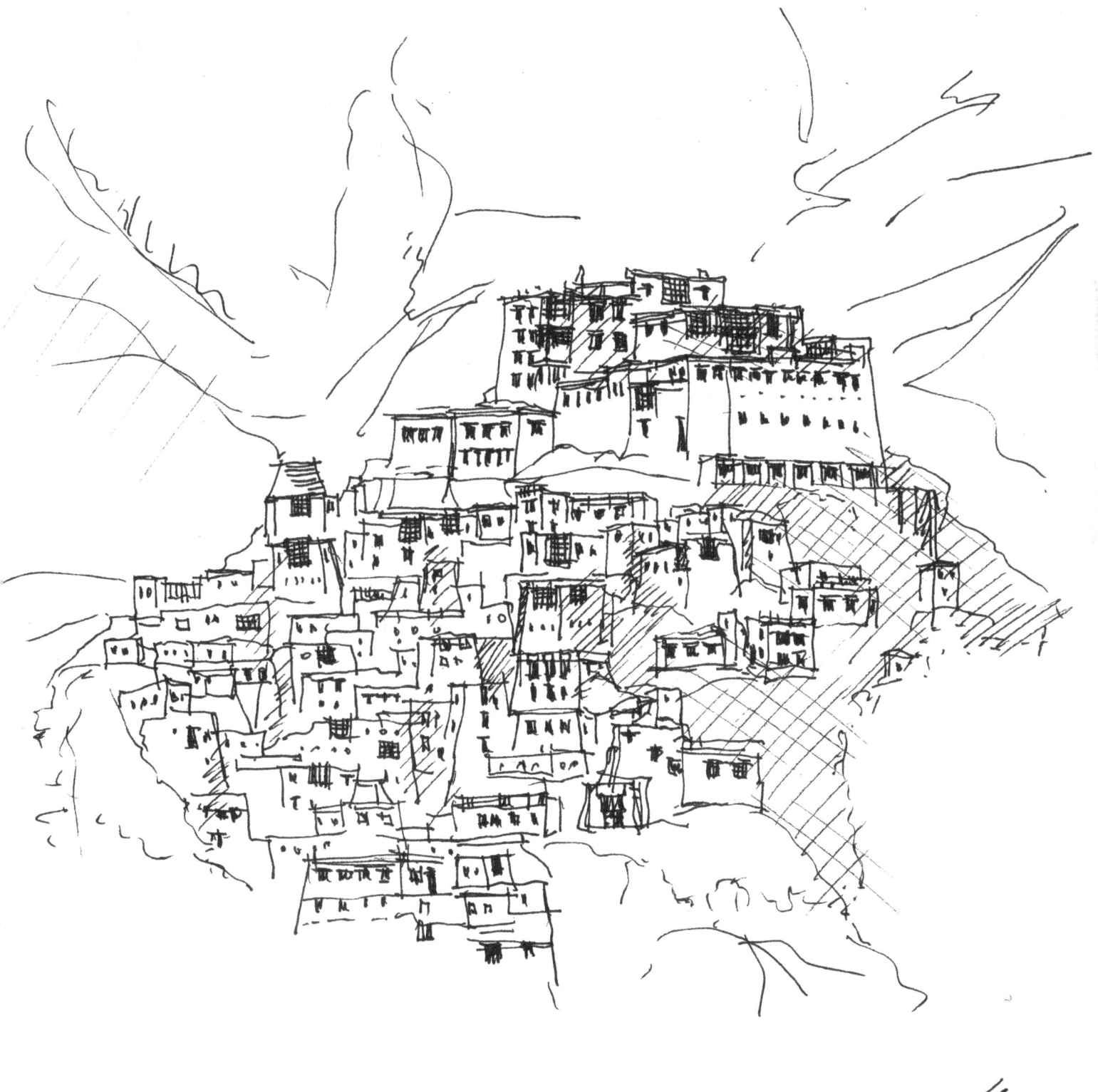

5. Stakna Gompa

The Buddhist monastery of Stakna is located about 25km from Leh, on the left bank of the Indus River. Was founded in the 16th century by the Bhutan teacher Chosje Jamyang Palkar. Being on the top of the steep hill and resembling to the top of the nose of tiger, is named "Tigers Nose."

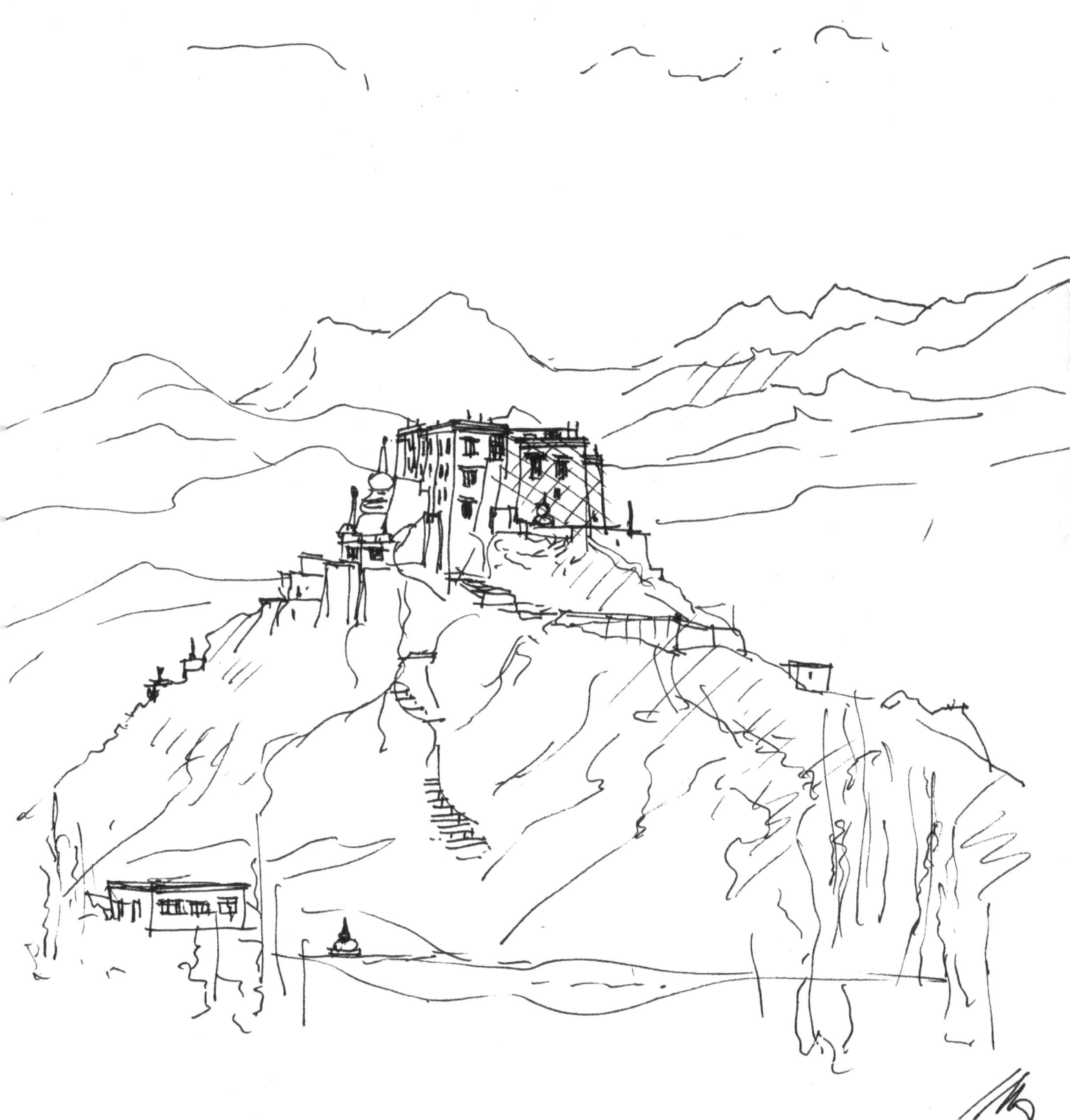

6. Lamayuru Gompa

One of the oldest monasteries in Ladakh, Lamayuru Gompa is situated about 125 km from the capital of Leh, on the way to Srinagar, built on a steep rock with a magnificent view. In the monastery are about 150 monks of the Buddhist branch "Red Hats." It is believed that in the past there were about 400 priests.

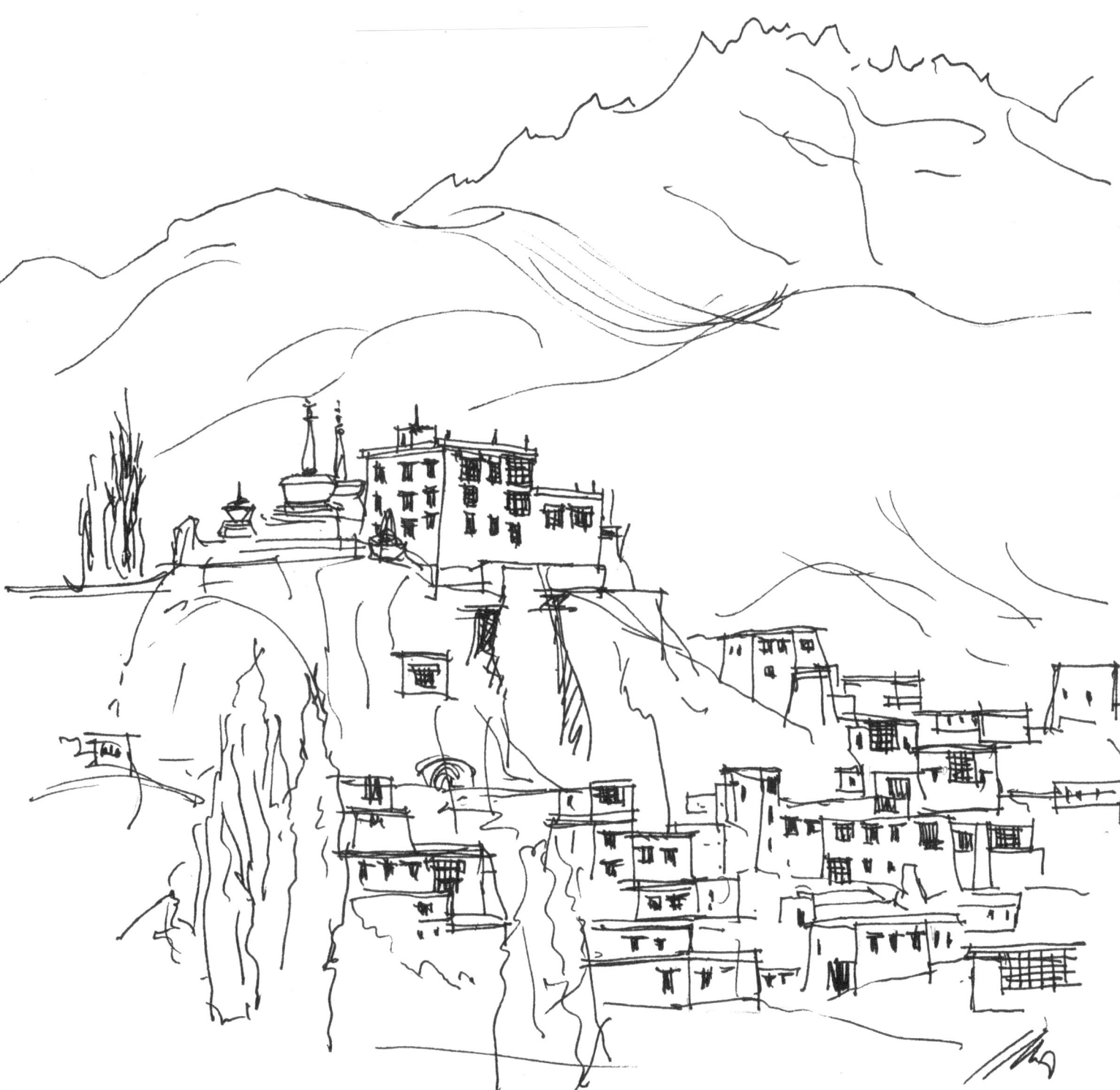

7. Namgyal Tsemo Gompa

This monastery was founded by King of Ladakh Tashi Namgyal in 1430. Built on a rock above the city of Leh and contains the golden statue of Maitreya Buddha three floors high.

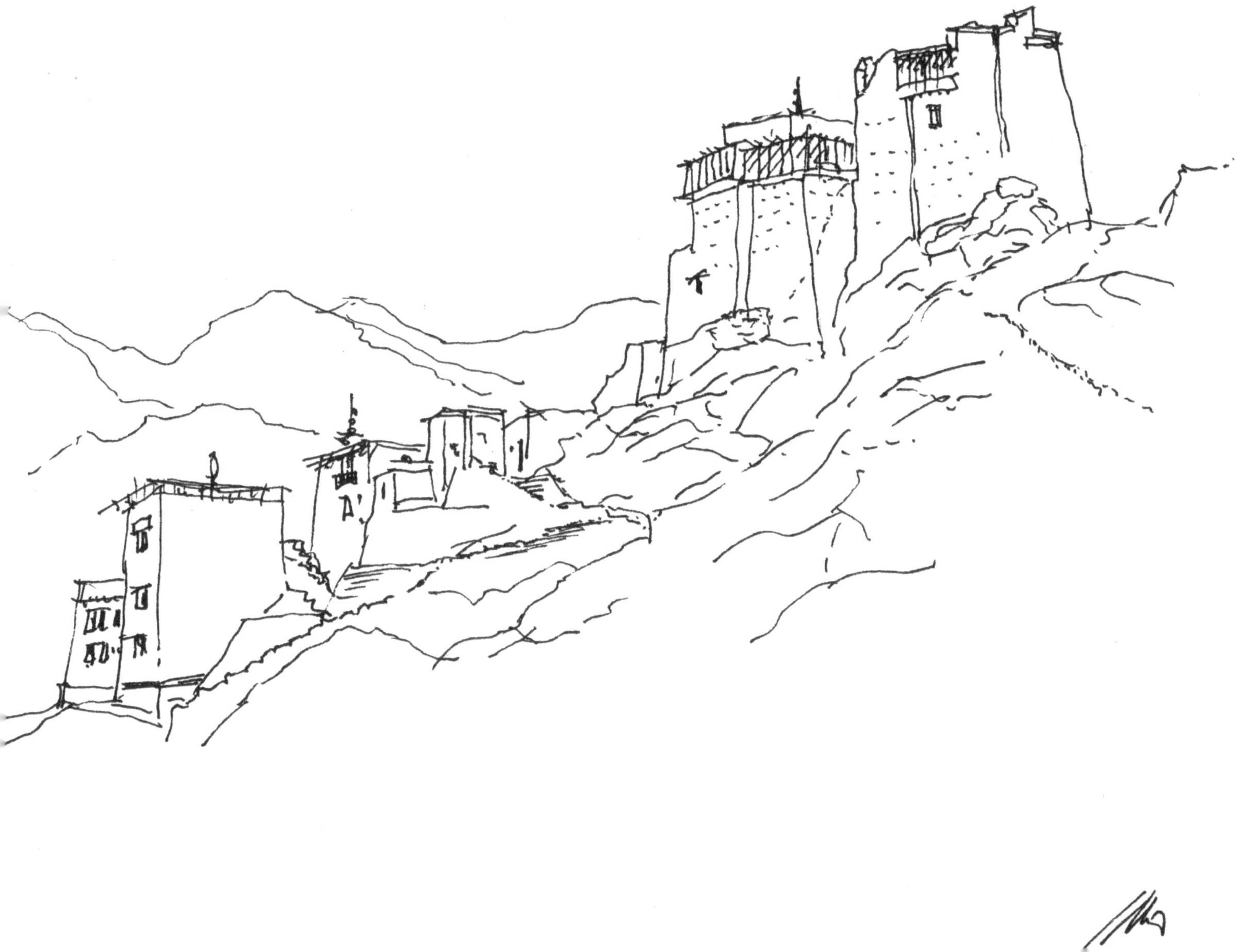

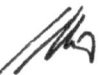

8. Spituk Gompa

About 100 monks live in this monastery near Leh. It contains the giant statue of the Hindu goddess Kali. Every year, the Gustor festival is held in the monastery.

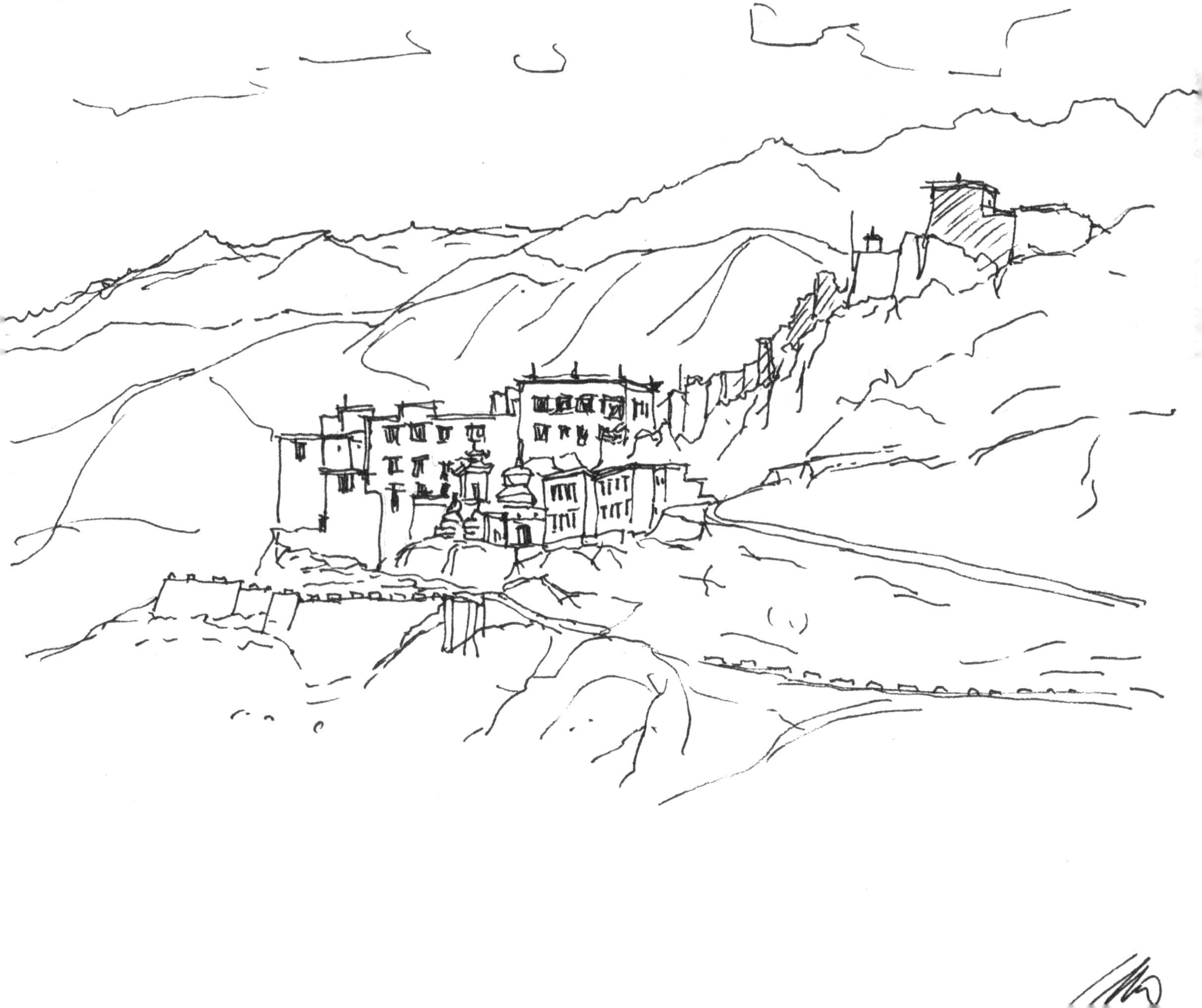

9. Thiksey Monastery

Thiksey Gompa is a monastery of the Buddhist Order Gelug, erected at the top of a hill above the Thiksey River, about 19 km east of Leh. The monastery was founded by Jangsem Sherab Zangpo, a student of Je Tsongkhapa, founder of the Gelug School, in 1433 as a small village monastery. During October-November is an annual festival known as Gustor ritual.

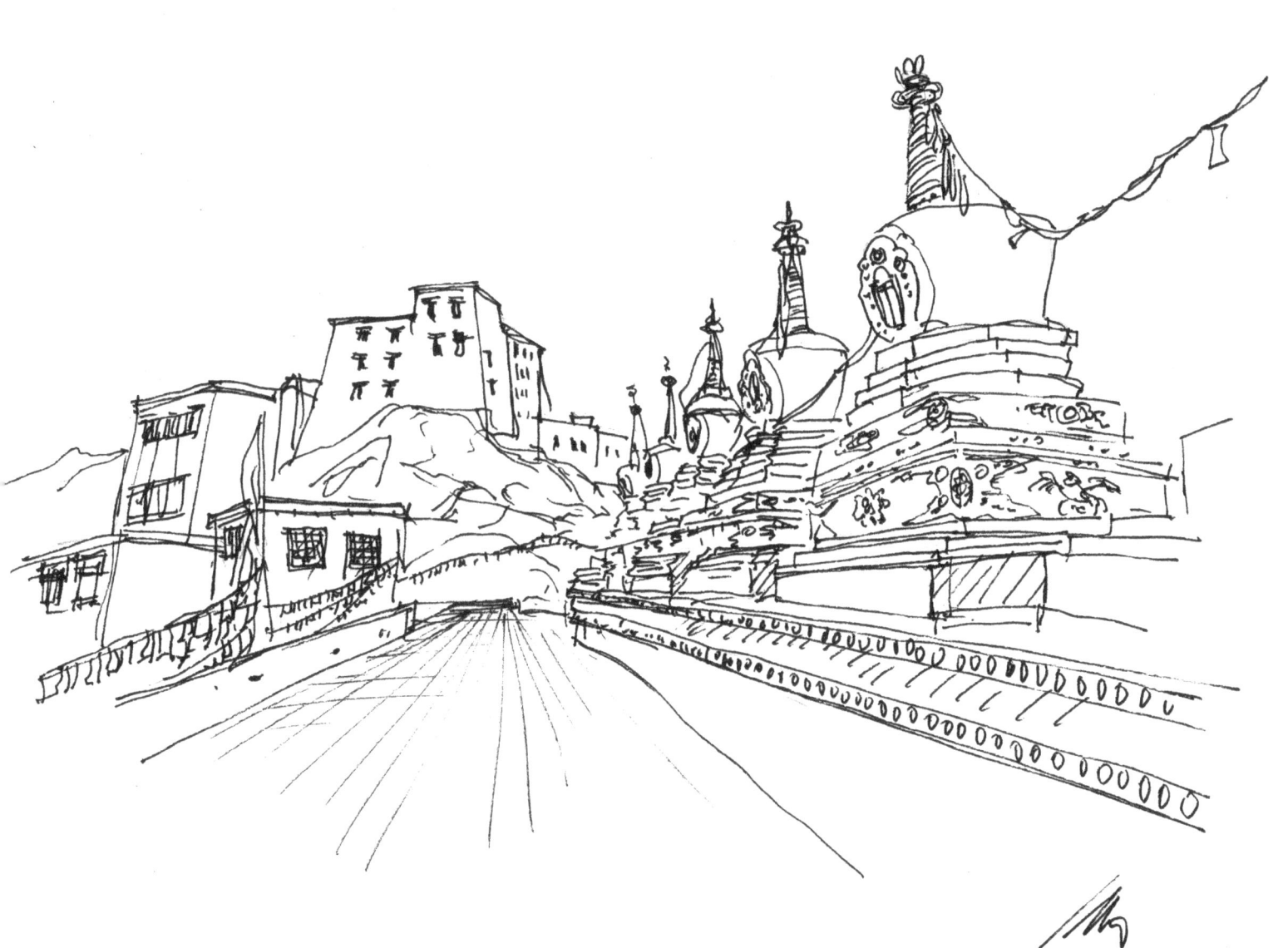

10. Stakna Gompa

Tourist little know about Stakna, Buddhist monastery erected on the hill fwith a wonderful view on Indus River valley,

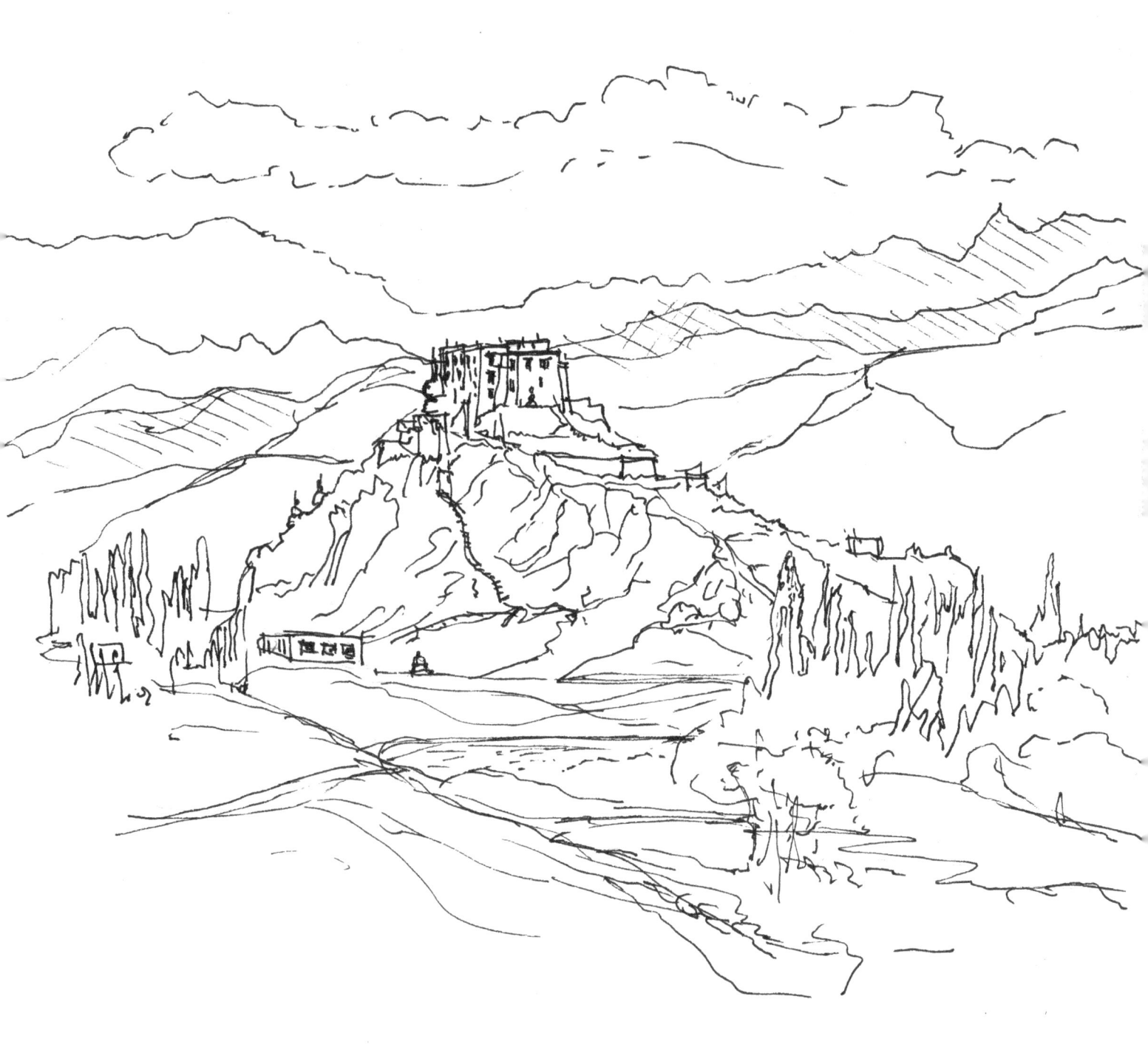

11. Cham dance, masked monk

Cham is a traditional dance among Tibetan Buddhists when masked and costumed dancers show moral instructions to spread the compassion to all conscious beings. Through Cham dance Buddhists pay tribute to every compassionate being.

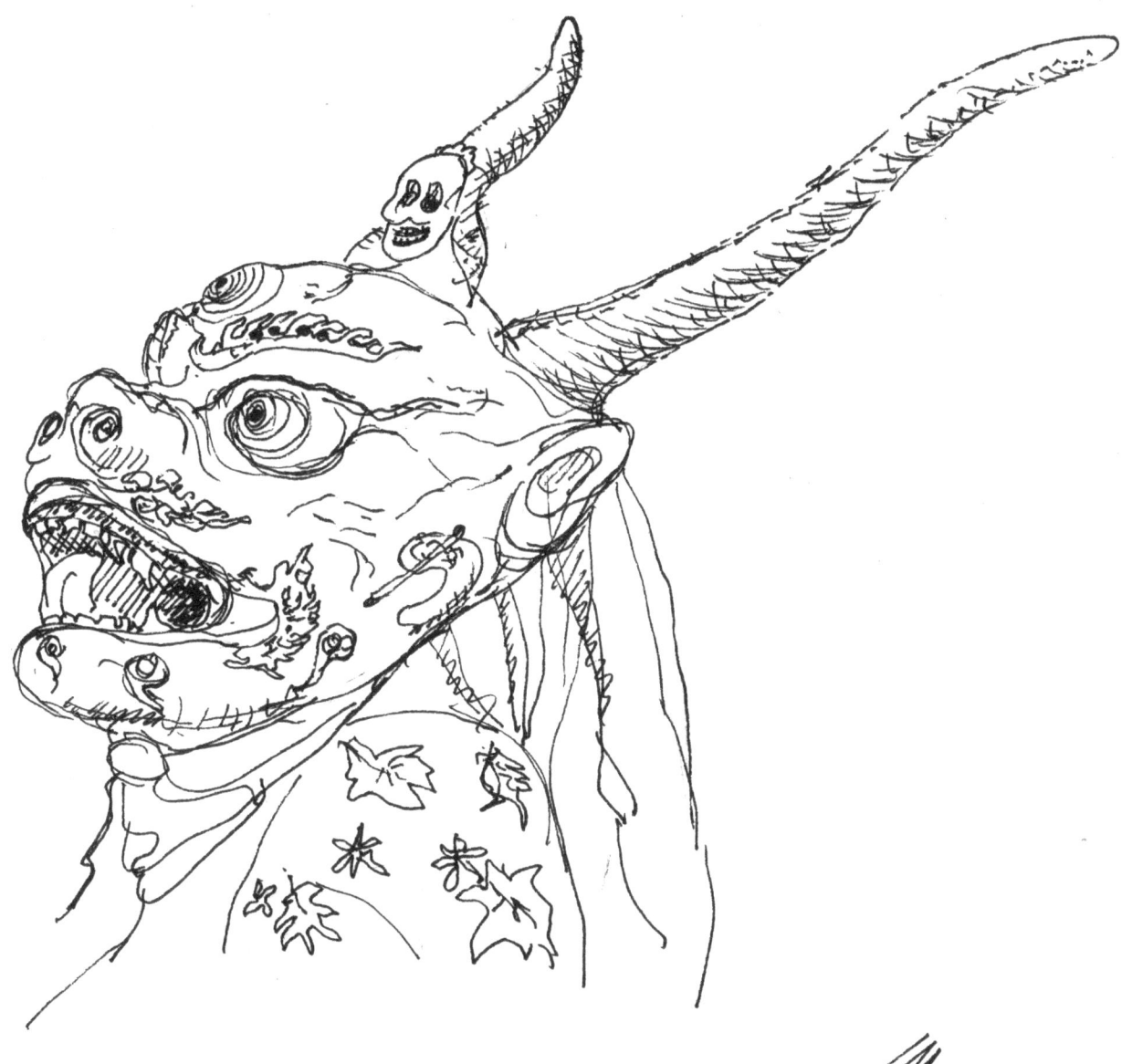

12. Lamayuru Gompa

Lamayuru Monastery was founded in the 10th century. It is believed that Lamayuru valley once was a lake, and after drying up became the fascinating place for building the Gompa. Today, most of the Buddhist settlement lies in ruins, and only the main Prayer hall is preserved.

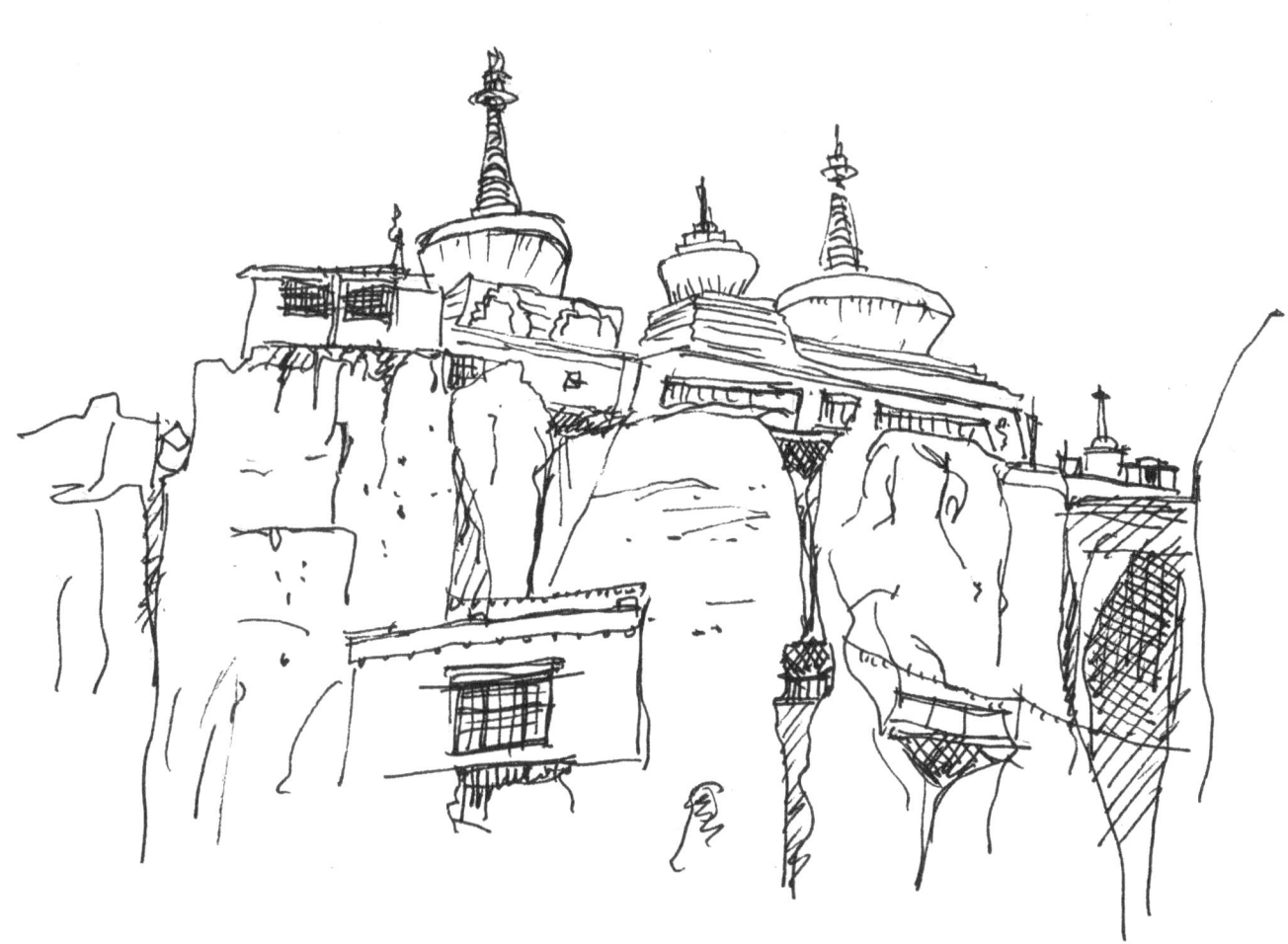

13. Namgyal Monastery

A look at Namgyal Gompa up the hill, high above Leh.

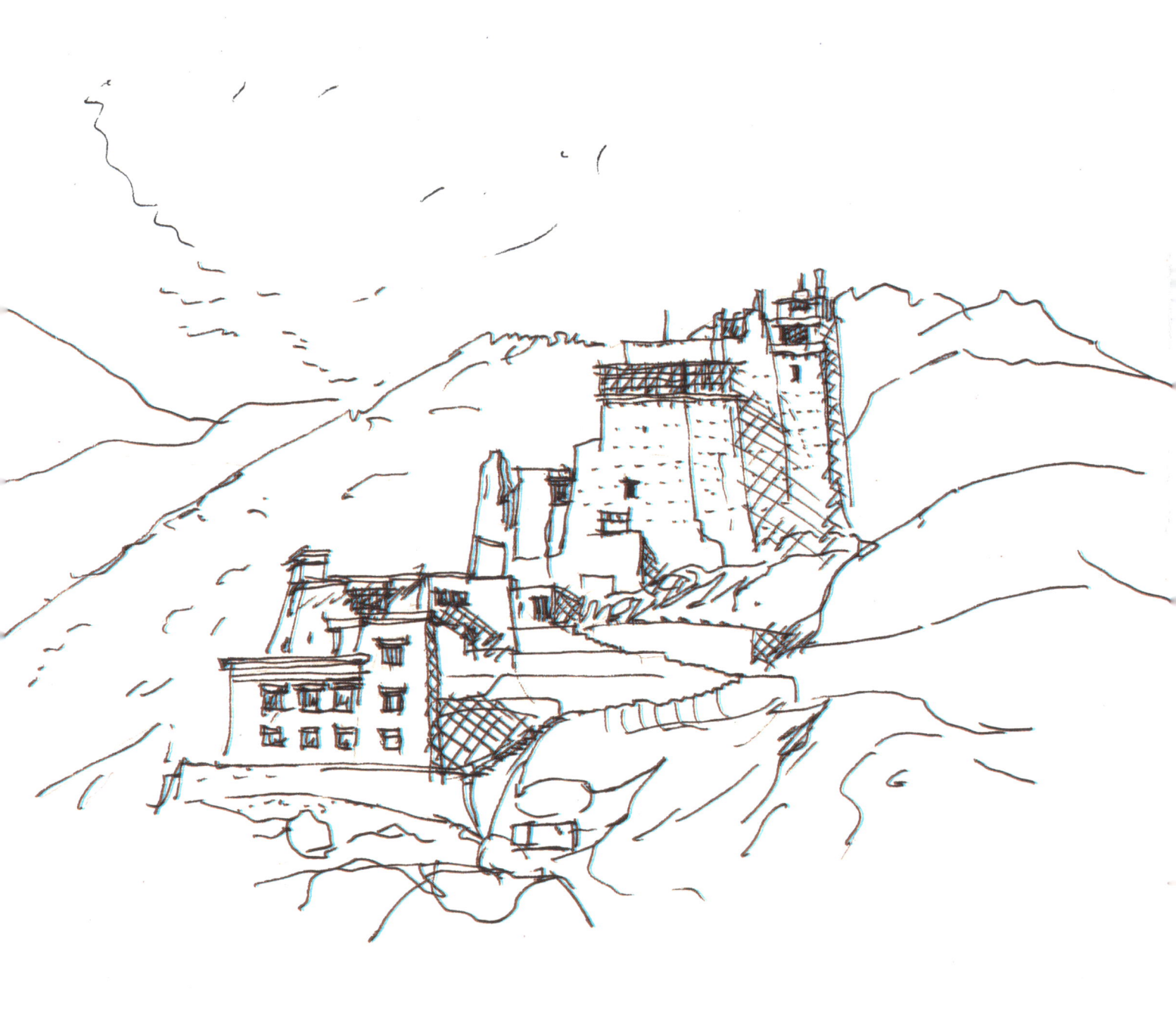

14. Making mandala

Spiritual and ritual symbol in Hinduism and Buddhism, mandala is a painting or spatial representation that symbolizes the Universe. This metaphysical or symbolic visual representation of microcosm and Universe is transmitted to observers through the art of making and destroying mandalas. Tibetan Buddhists make a mandala placing colored sand on a horizontal flat surface, producing a complex geometric form of Buddhist Pure Land. Mandala creation lasts several days. After finishing the mandala, Buddhist monks destroy it, an this act symbolizes total transience.

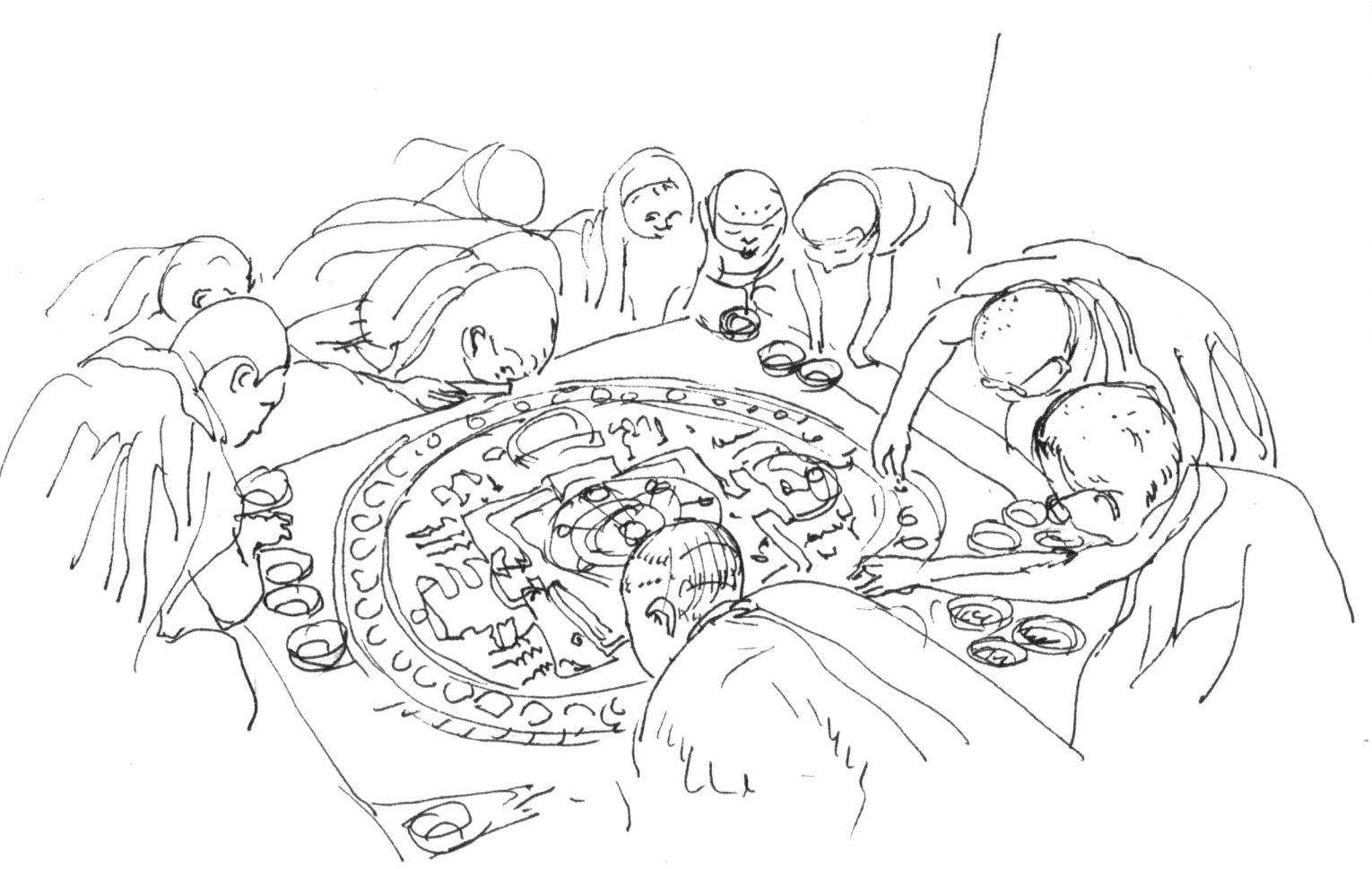

15. Shey Old Palace

Shey Gompa and the Shey Palace complex are located on the hill above the village of Shey, about 15 km south of Leh. In the past, Shey's Old Palace was the summer residence of the king, built by King of Ladakh Deldan Namgyal in 1655. The Palace is an integral part of the larger complex, which belongs to destroyed fortress and monastery.

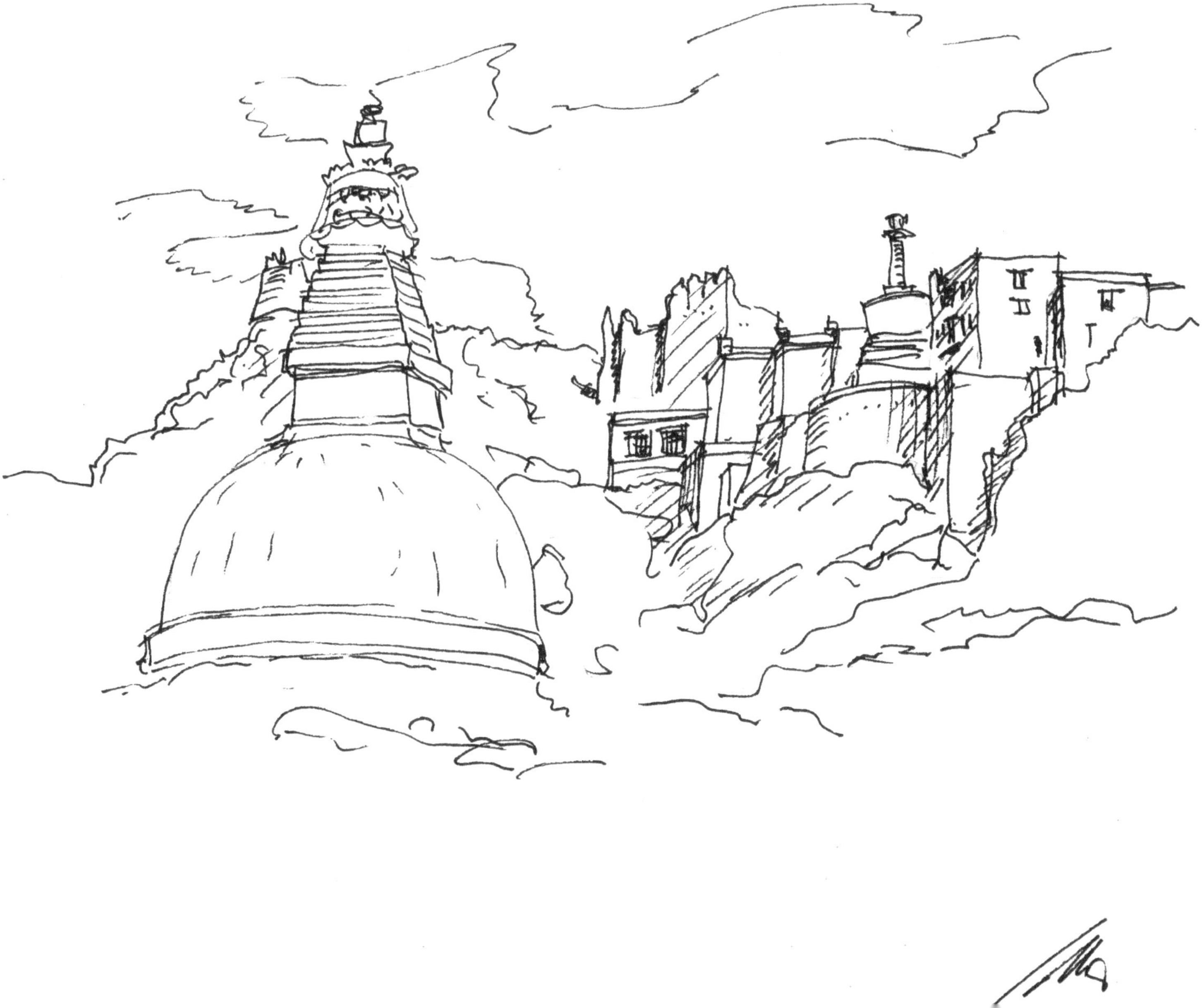

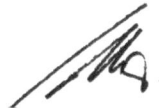

16. Bardan Gompa, Zanskar

Bardan Gompa is located in the Zanskar Valley, about 12 km from Padum. Founded in the 16th century, this is one of the oldest monasteries in Zanskar and belongs to the Drukpa branch of the Kagyu school of Tibetan Buddhism. Today there are about 45 monks living in this gompa.

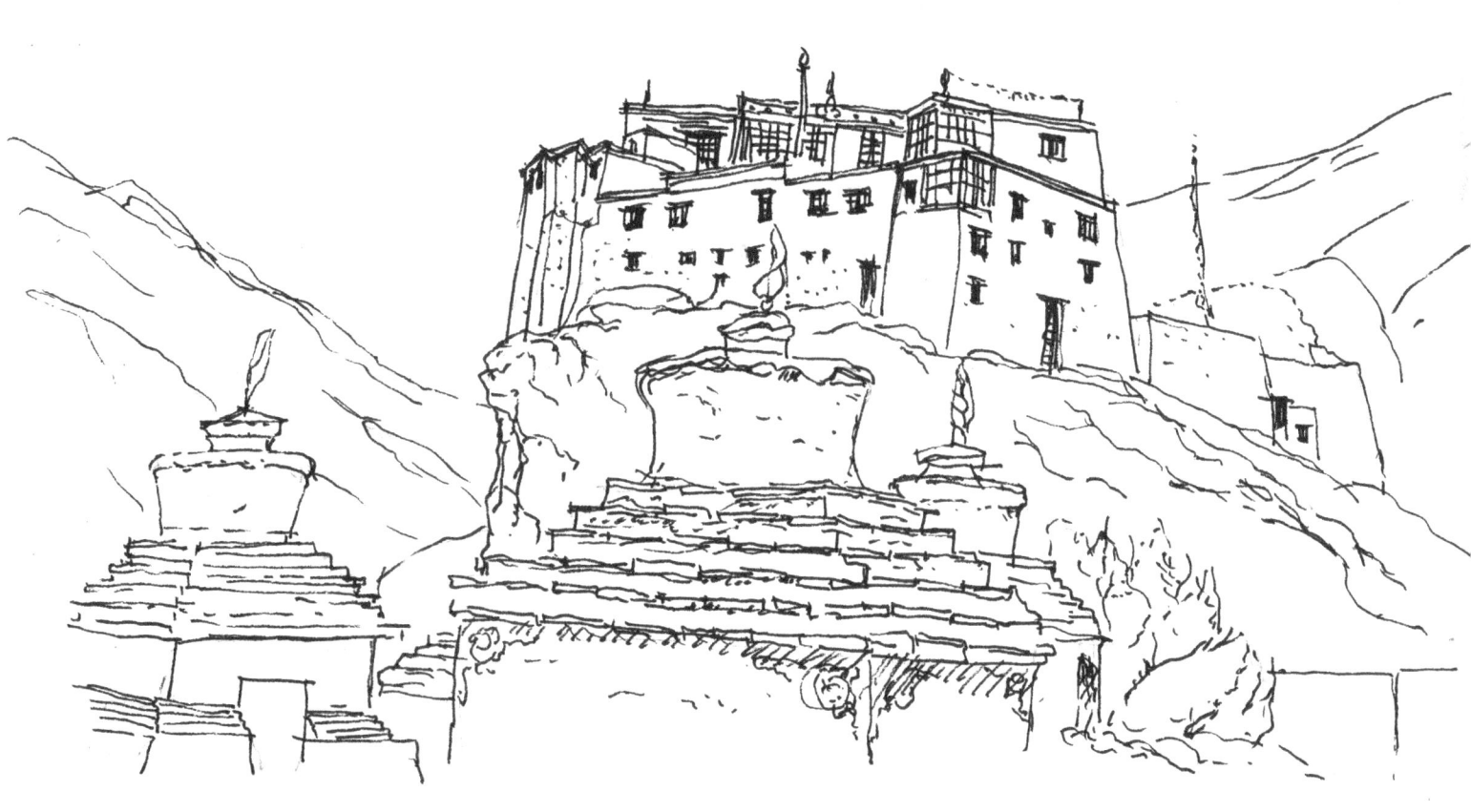

17. Lamayuru Monastery

A view of the Lamayuru Gompa on the hill, just below.

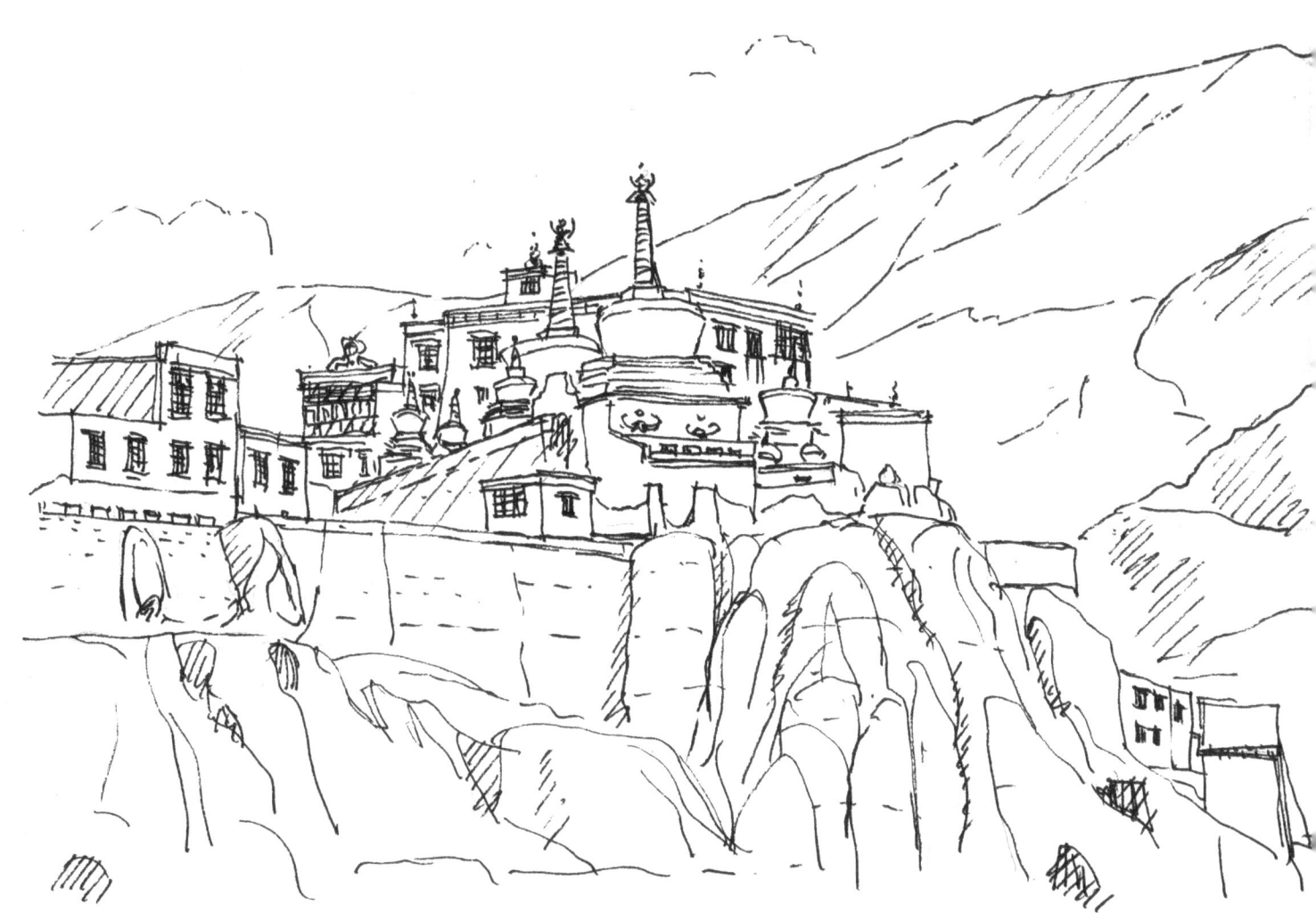

18. Leh Palace, Leh

The Leh Palace was built in 1553 and was completed in the 17th century. Construction of the palace began king Tsewang Namgyal and finished Sennge Namgyal, both from the Namgyal dynasty. Built as a royal palace, it dominates above the city of Leh. Designed by the ideal model of Potala Palace in Lhasa, Tibet, built in a smaller scale.

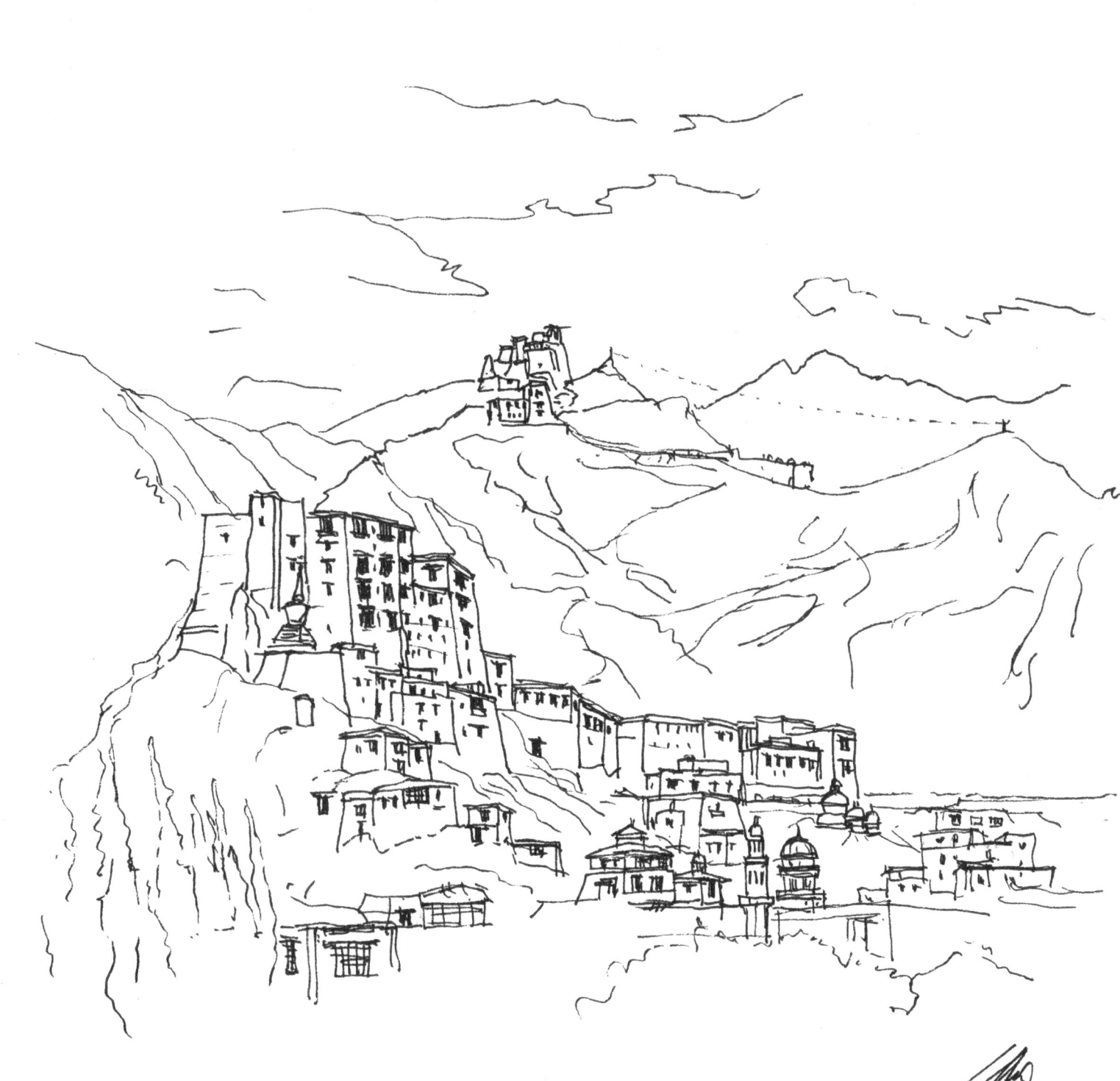

19. Lamayuru Gompa

Lamayuru Gompa is older than 1100 years. It is the monastery of Drikung Kagyu lineage of Tibetan Buddhism. For centuries this monastery has been appreciated for excellence in practical training of meditation, and has always been home to mystics and mysticism.

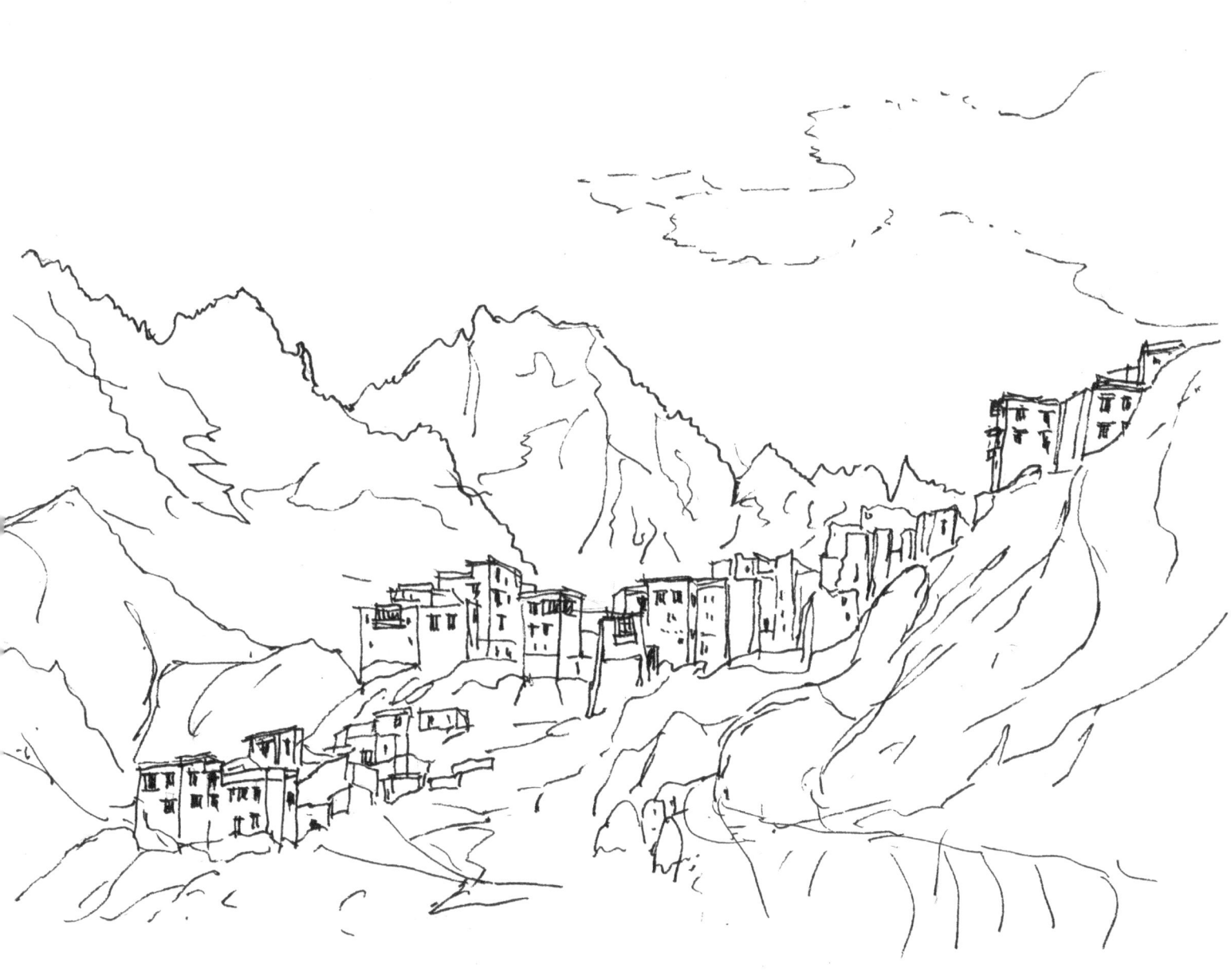

20. Stupas nearby Shey Gompa

Nearby Shey Gompa there are many stupas.

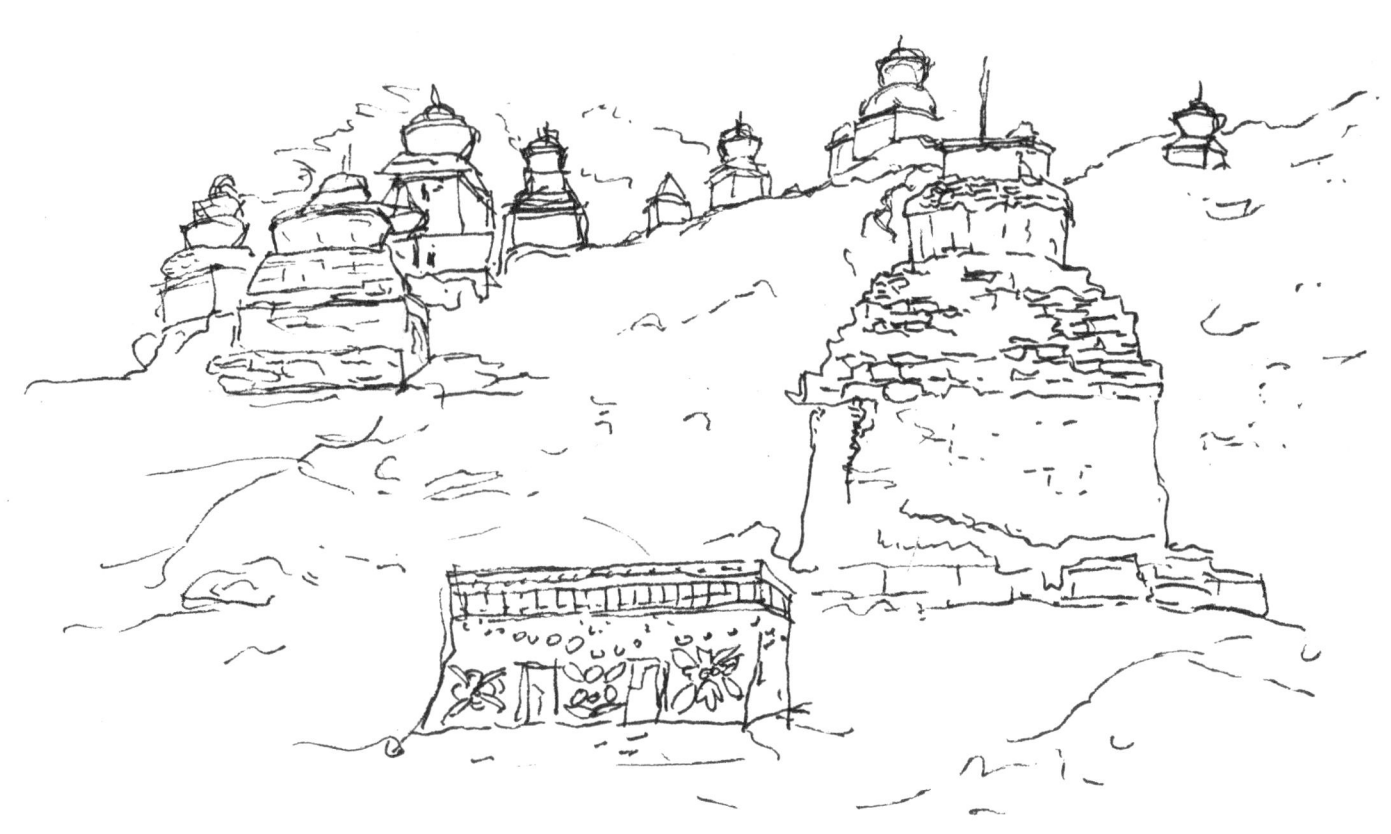

21. Cham dance, Leh

Traditional Cham dance under masks originates from the 8th century and is held every year in Ladakh monasteries. It is believed Cham dance brings happiness and benefit to those who watch this dance.

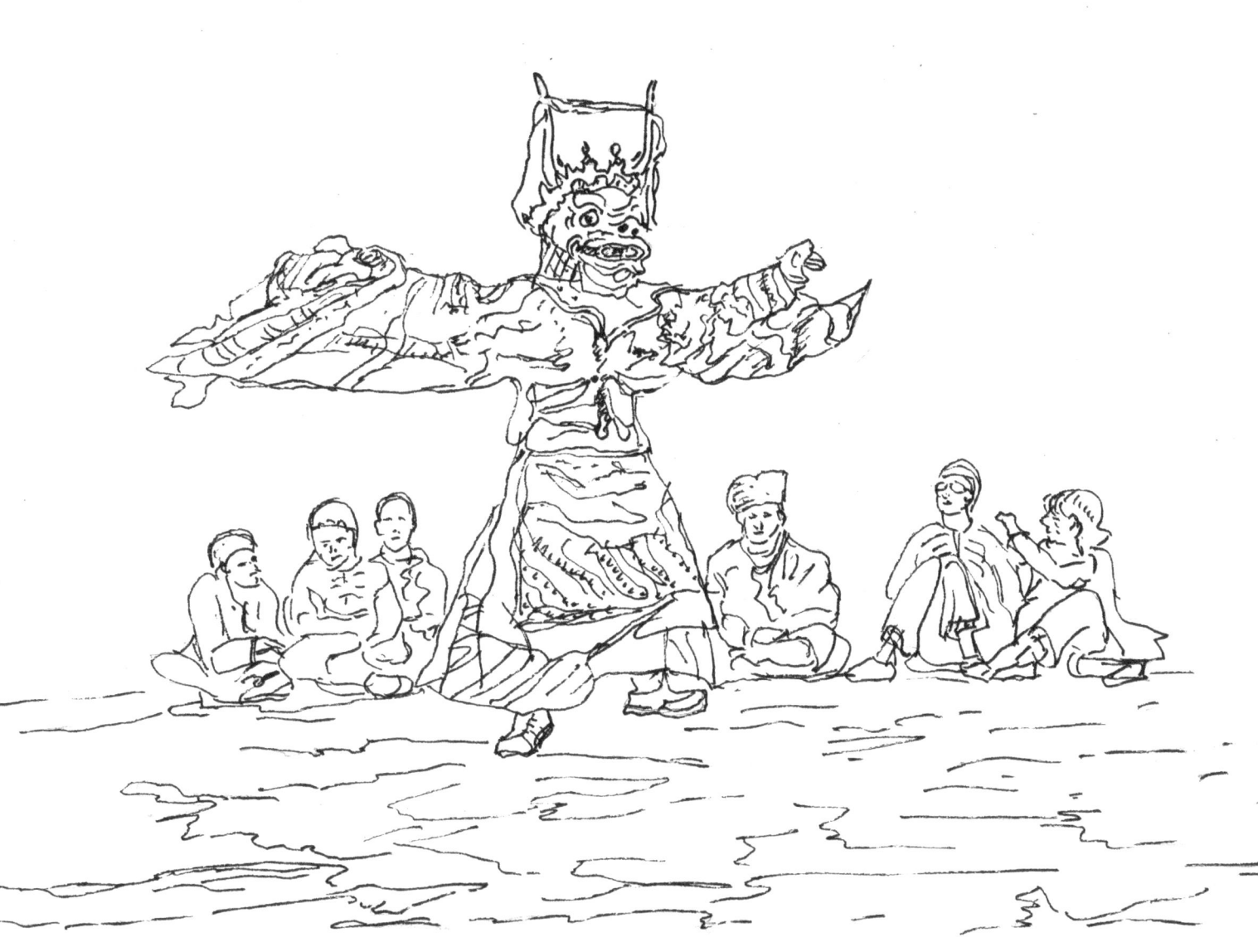

22. Monk playing lawah - long trumpet

Lawah is a long trumpet, a wind instrument used in Buddhist monasteries in Ladakh. Buddhist monks play this long trumpet during a puja ritual, when offerings are made to Buddha.

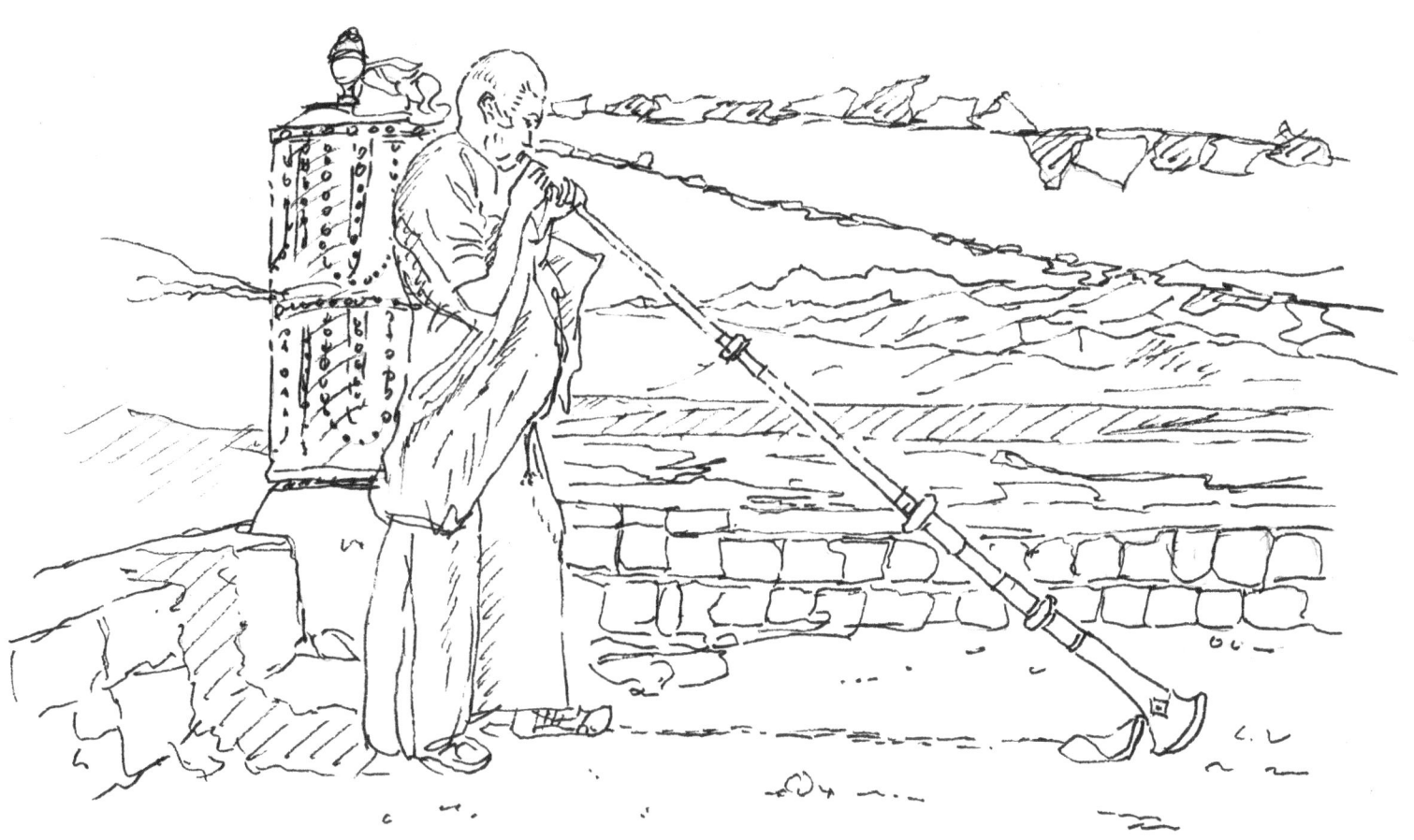

23. Boy monk at Thiksey Gompa

A boy monk spinning a prayer wheel at Thiksey Gompa. Prayer wheel is a cylindrical metal wheel set at the accessory of Buddhist temple with a relief inscription of mantra "Om Mani Padme Hum" written in Sanskrit. According to the Buddhist tradition, the turning of the prayer wheel with the simultaneous recitation of mantras significantly increases its power.

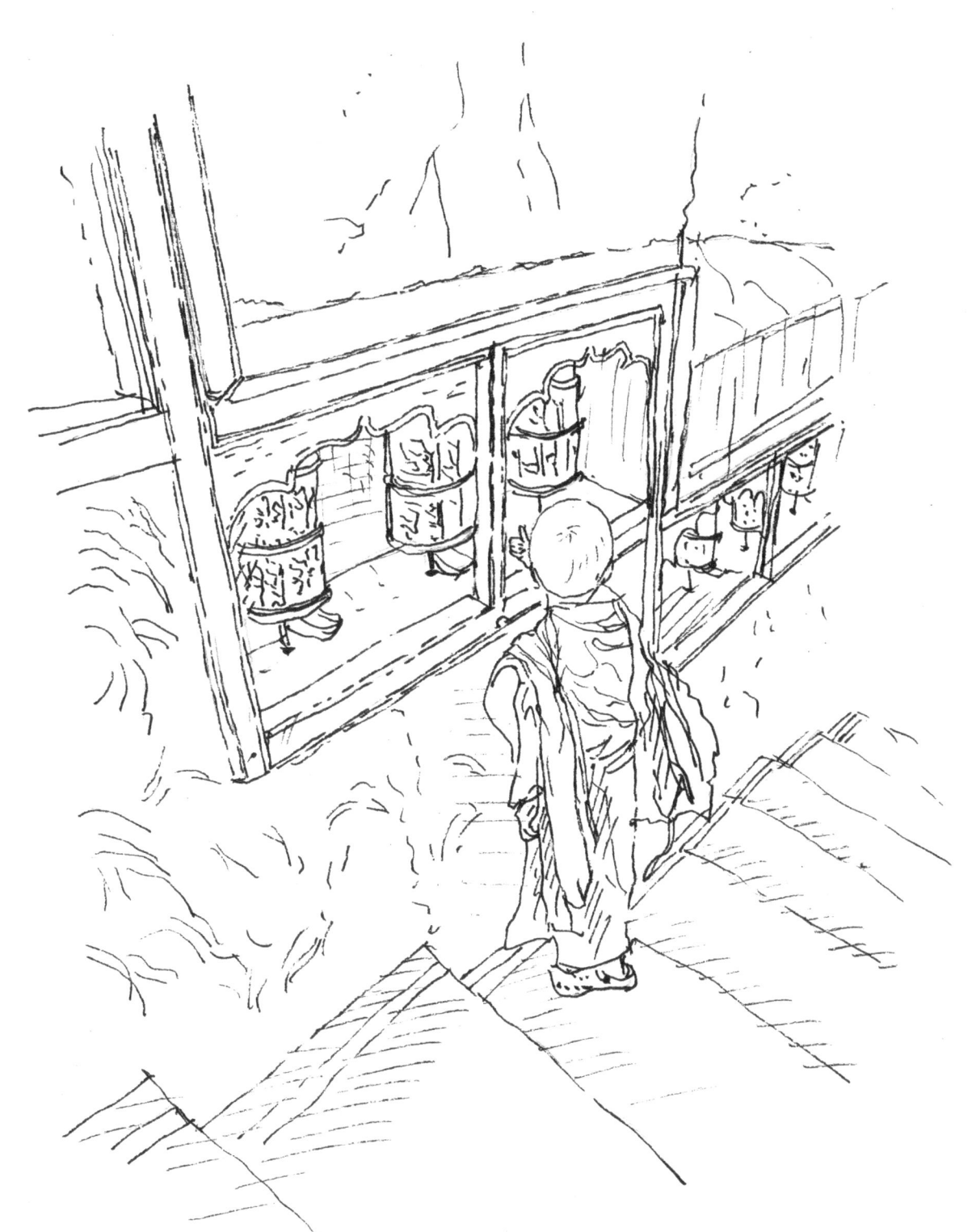

24. Diskit Gompa, Nubra valley

This gompa belongs to the Gelugpa (Yellow Hats) school of Tibetan Buddhism, located in the Nubra Valley. Diskit Gompa was founded in the 14th century by Changzem Tserab Zangpo, a student of the famous Tibetan Buddhist teacher Tsong Khapa. Diskit Gompa is built on the top of the hill above the plains of Shyok River, which runs parallel to the Indus River. River valley was once a trade route between Tibet and China.

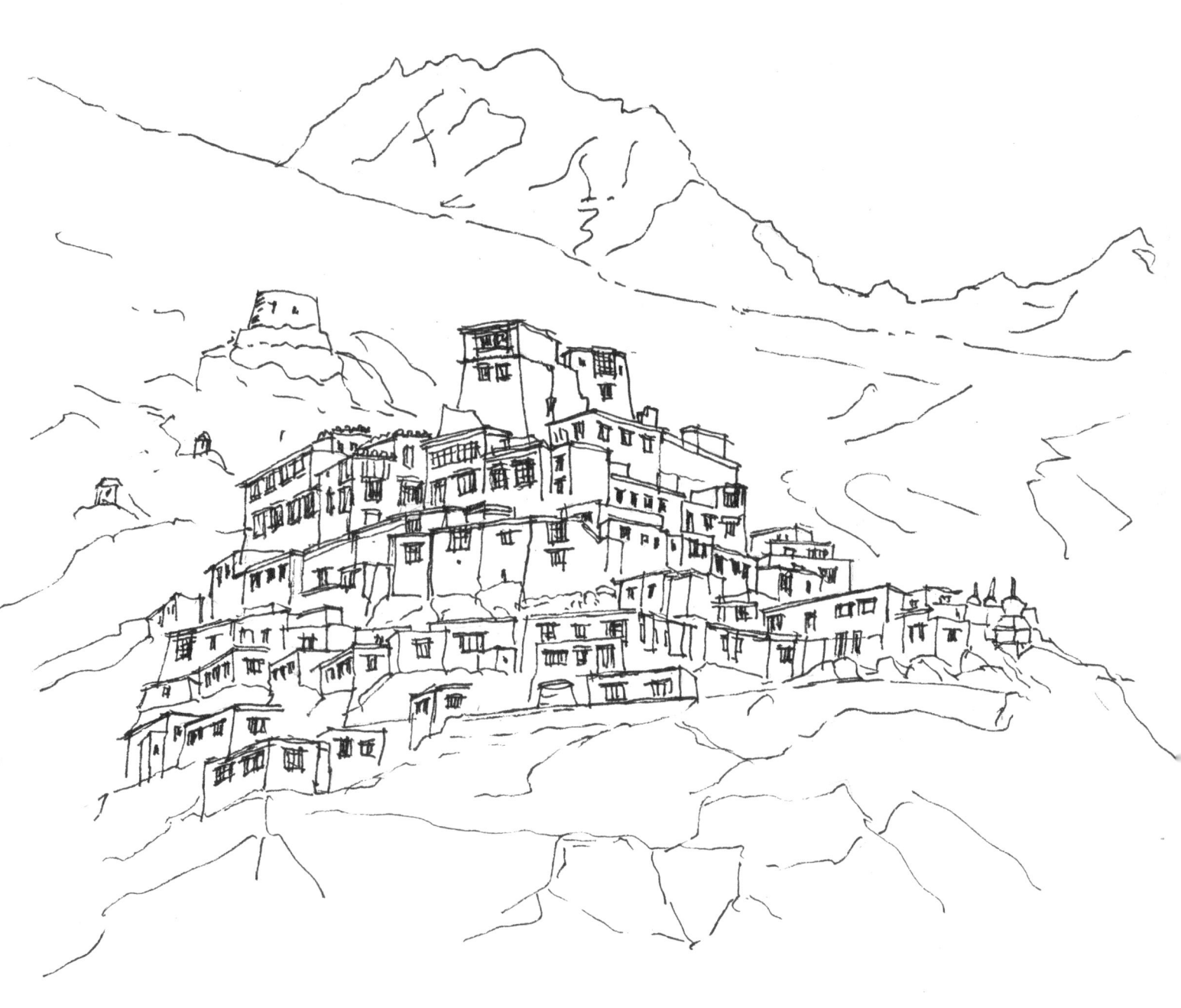

25. Diskit Gompa

Diskit Gompa inhabits approximately hundred monks containing a school for Tibetan children. Monastery hosts annual festival called Desmochhey, also known as the "Festival of the scapegoat," during which is represented superiority of the good over bad forces.

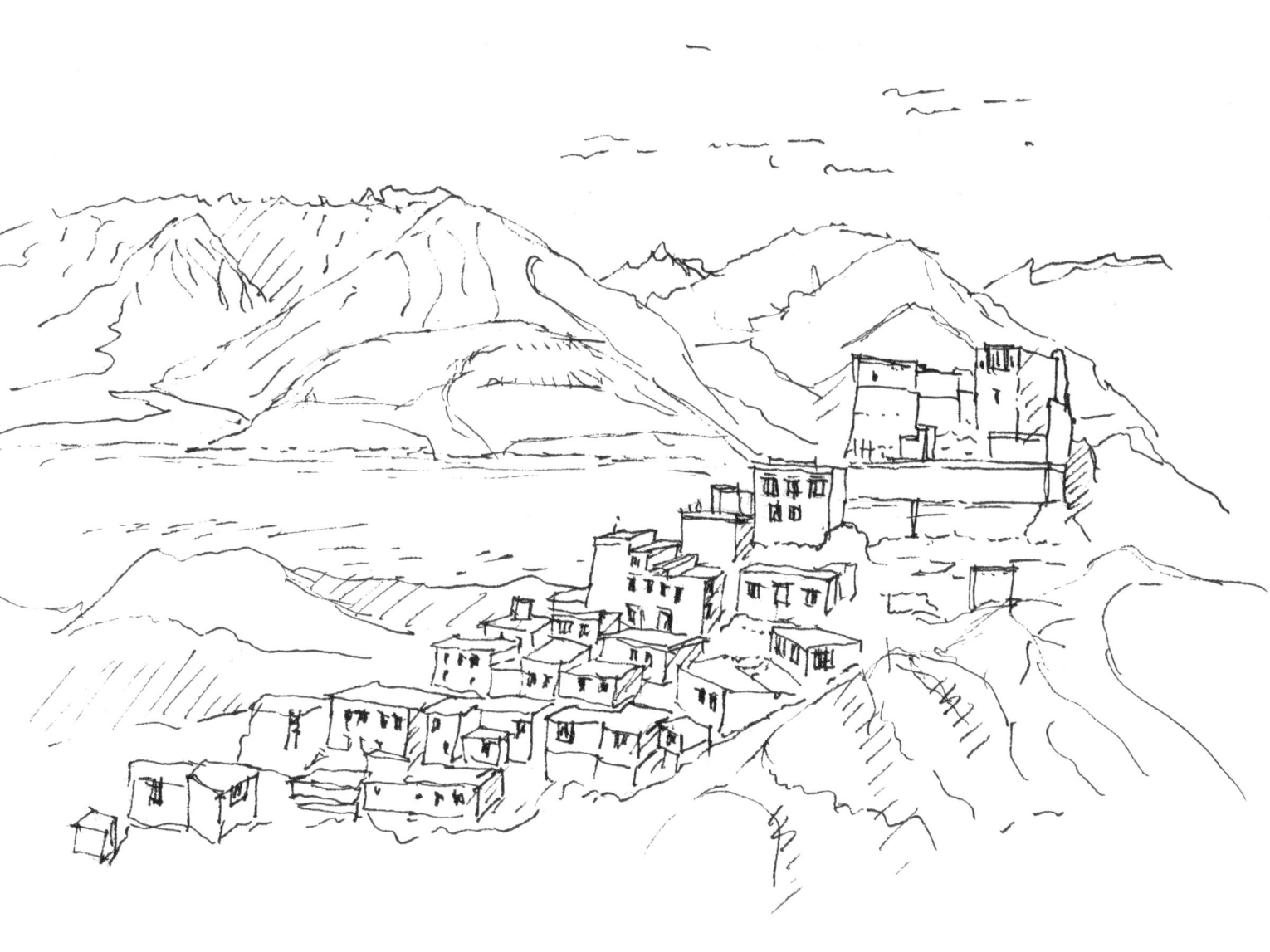

26. Basgo Gompa

Basgo gompa was built in 1680 in the village of Basgo, about 40km away from Leh. In the past, was an important cultural center. It is located on the top of a hill, above the ruins of the former settlement.

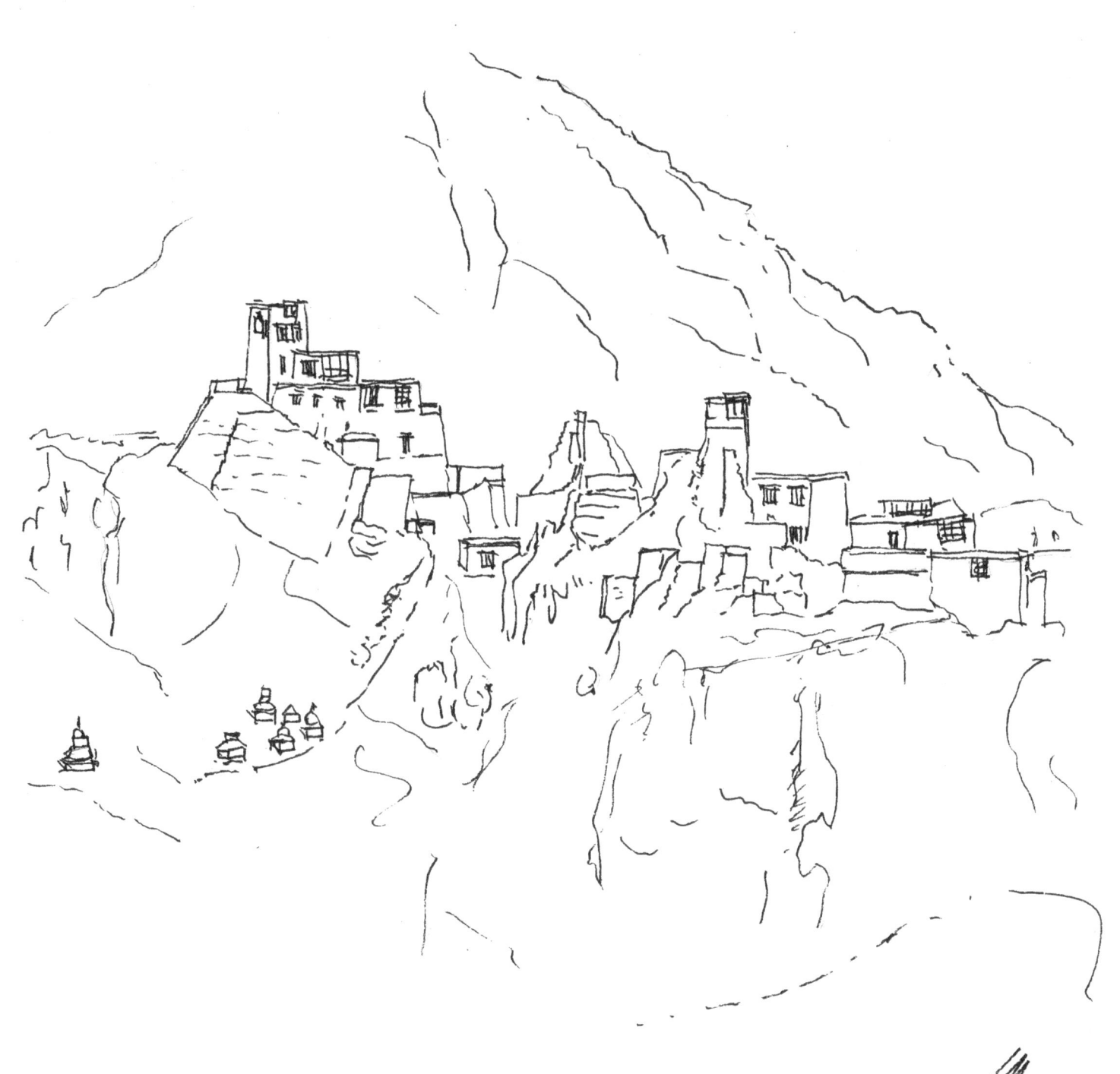

27. Buddhist stupas in Ladakh

In Ladakh are built thousands of Buddhist stupas (chortens). The square base of the chorten symbolizes earth, the dome symbolizes water, and the Steps of the Enlightenment where it rests symbolize the element of fire. At the top of the column is a parasol, a wind symbol covering the sphere with a familiar "double symbol" that unites the Sun and the Moon and represents the glittering Crown of chorten.

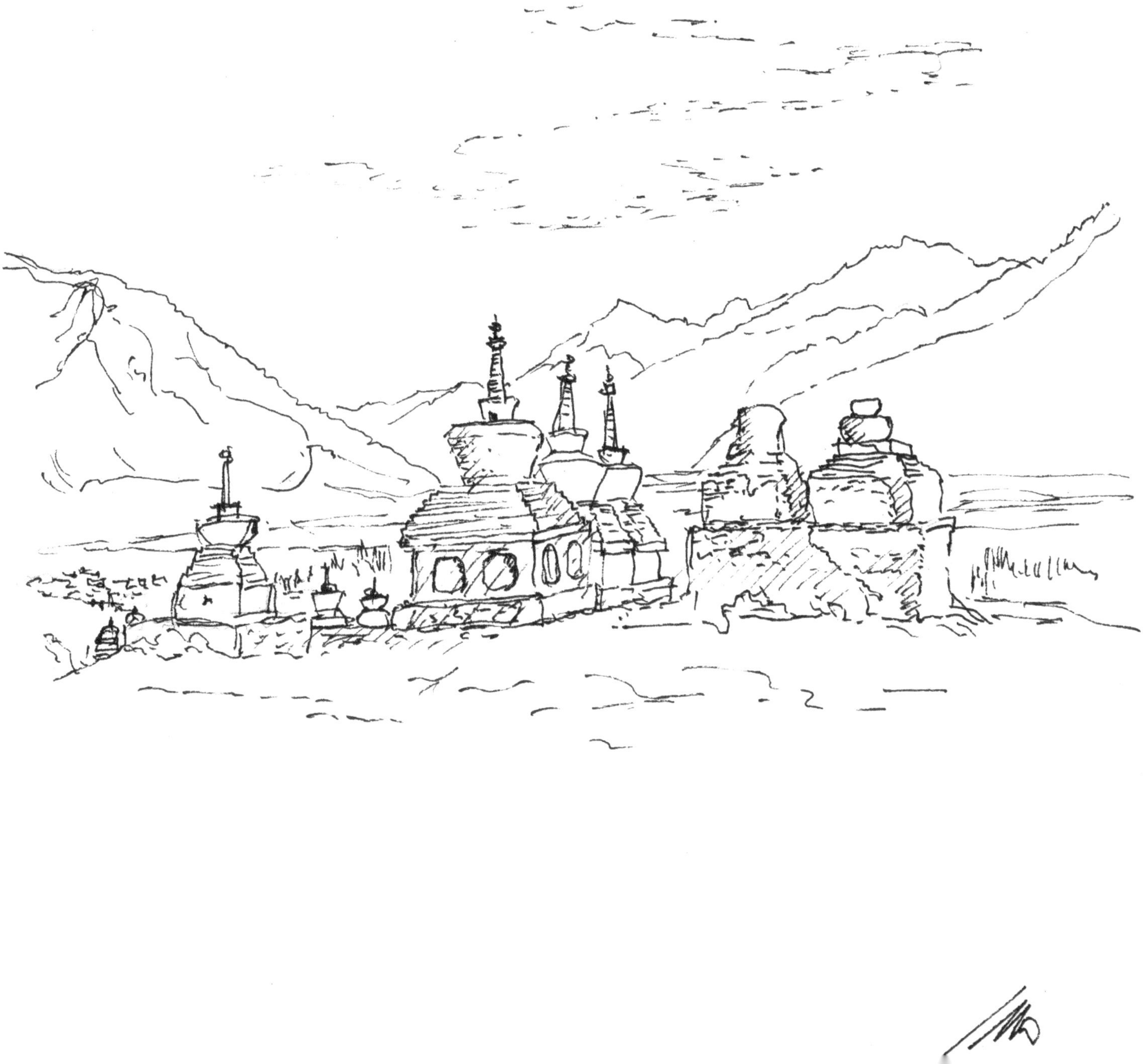

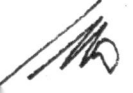

28. Buddhist monk performing Cham dance

A costumed Buddhist priest with a mask representing the head of a deer dancing Cham dance.

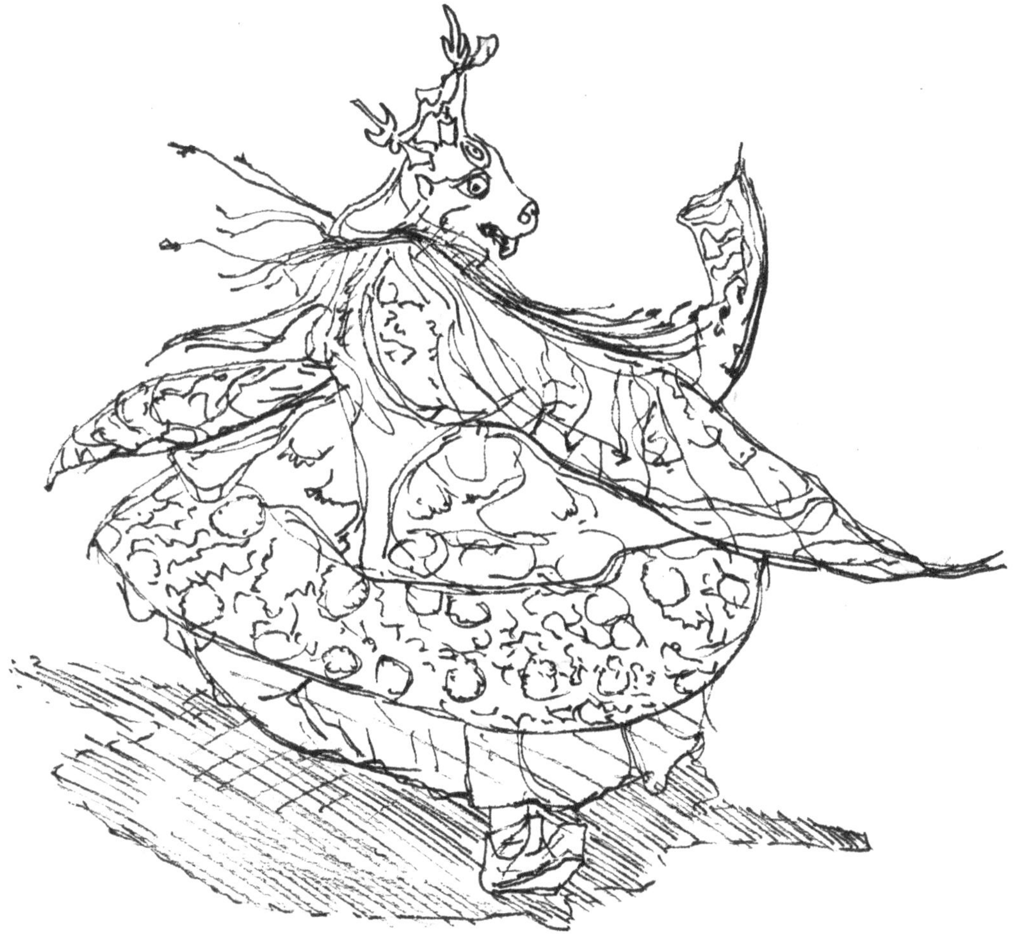

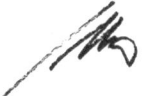

29. Shey Palace, detail of facade

The architecture of Shey Palace is characterized by wooden balconies made in traditional Tibetan style.

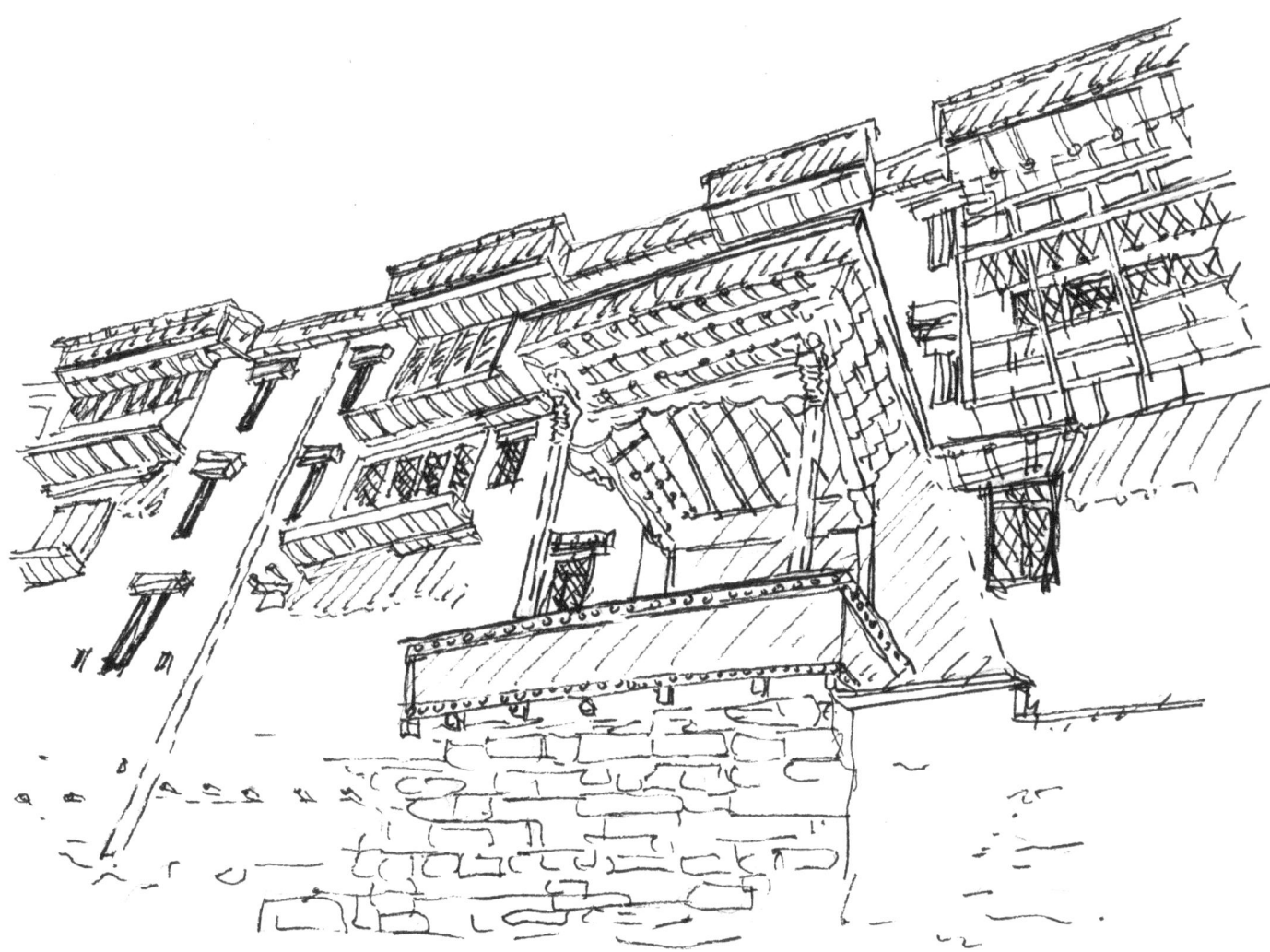

30. Buddhist monks meditating, Soma Gompa, Leh

Meditation is an ancient Buddhist practice that carries the roots of Buddhist philosophy. Meditation develops concentration, inner peace and insight into one's own consciousness. In all Buddhist monasteries meditation is a daily practice.

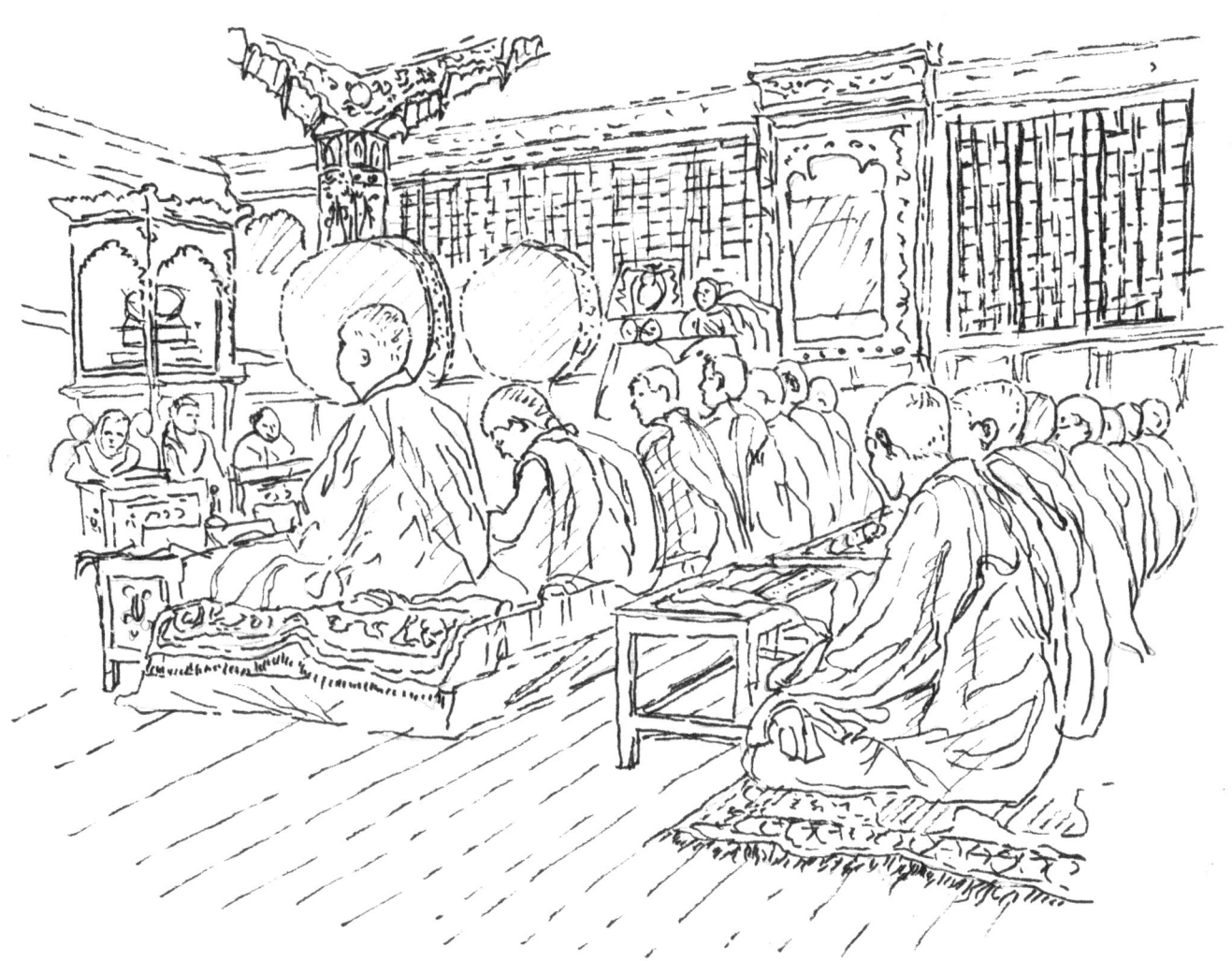

www.ingramcontent.com/pod-product-compliance
Lightning Source LLC
Chambersburg PA
CBHW051201220526
45473CB00003B/857